Lost and Found in London

Peter - I'm thrilled to share my own life-enhancing journey with someone who is here thanks to a "miracle!"

I wish you nothing but positive, eye-opening travels in 2014... and beyond.

Kathleen

Lost and Found in London

How the Railway Tracks Hotel Changed Me

Kathleen O'Hara

Copyright © 2011 by Kathleen O'Hara.

First Edition
Cover Photos: Chris Harvey/Micky Absil

Library of Congress Control Number: 2011914775
ISBN: Hardcover   978-1-4653-3855-6
               Softcover   978-1-4653-3854-9
               Ebook   978-1-4653-3856-3

All rights reserved. No part of this book may be reproduced or transmitted in any form or by any means, electronic or mechanical, including photocopying, recording, or by any information storage and retrieval system, without permission in writing from the copyright owner.

"This book is based on my own experiences. However, I have made changes to enhance the story and protect certain people. Any errors are mine, not theirs."

This book was printed in the United States of America.

To order additional copies of this book, contact:
Xlibris Corporation
1-888-795-4274
www.Xlibris.com
Orders@Xlibris.com

For Wren, Mum, George Whitman, and Tony Benn

And for progressive activists—wherever you may be—who are seeking to change yourselves, the world, or both.

PROLOGUE

It was one of those life-changing encounters that could so easily have been missed. All it took was the lift doors not doing what they were supposed to do—stay closed.

I got on alone, pushed the button; the doors shut tight, and I prepared to descend. But didn't. Instead, the doors suddenly opened again; and there he was, a dark stranger, looming.

"Oh," was all I could say. Then I rallied and added, wittily, I hoped, "I think there's room for more."

"How fortunate," he said, smiling.

The stranger stepped into the lift as I moved slightly to one side.

This time, the doors stayed closed, and we began our short trip down. That's when I recognized him from the conference on 21st Century Issues I had just attended—one of many events at the London School of Economics that inspired the writer/activist/intellectual wannabe in me.

He was the rugged, yet distinguished-looking—always an intriguing combination—leader of a dynamic workshop on war and peace I'd participated in. Under his smooth direction, words like "internationalism," "disarmament," and "sustainability" had been tossed about with impressive ease.

And later during the general assembly, he had interrupted the chair to stop his babbling. "Jeremy," he'd said from the back of the lecture hall, "it might be time to give someone else a turn to speak."

Daring man, I thought. Obviously, he wasn't new to the gathering—as I was.

More to the point, he'd been right. Well-intentioned Jeremy had begun to bore us all.

For about five seconds, this striking fellow and I stood side by side in the lift, surrounded by the uncomfortable silence typical of the British in closed public spaces. Then he spoke. "I liked what you said in the workshop . . . about valuing others."

I laughed awkwardly, taken aback because he recognized me too, even though my contribution had been quite modest. The lift was beginning to feel tiny—almost filled—by the tall human being next to me.

"I guess I've always been a people person," I responded, a little too chirpily. "Even when I was a toddler, I'd say 'Hi' to everyone we passed in the street."

"I can see that," he said.

It was tempting to add that being outgoing wasn't as easy as it used to be. Too many men think you are flirting. Of course, that didn't prevent me from chatting there and then with someone I barely knew!

"It's a welcome change in this city," he added quietly.

"Oh, I find most people here quite friendly, very warm and generous."

"Perhaps they're responding to you. My name is Chris."

By the time we reached the ground, we had agreed to head to the nearest wine bar. Continue the conversation. I suggested a charming historic spot two blocks away, clearly impressing Chris with my intimate knowledge of his city.

"I thought I knew every building in central London, but this one is new for me," he said, ducking his head to climb down the narrow stairs leading to the dimly lit bar. "Thanks for expanding my horizons."

We found a quiet nook under the low, almost-claustrophobic ceiling in the back and soon our words flowed easily and openly, as if we were long-lost chums. We gossiped about people who had either delighted or irritated us at the conference with their views on war, peace, human rights, climate change, and were pleasantly surprised by how similar our reactions had been.

This person's comments were silly. Yes, I thought so. That one's were brilliant. They certainly were. Anyone watching us from afar would have seen two heads nodding vigorously—and frequently.

Halfway through the second glass of wine, I heard myself telling Chris that I had been given a deadline to leave the country. In little more than two weeks, I had to go into what felt like exile because I had stayed the maximum time allotted (a mere half year) for foreigners.

On top of that, the flat where I had lived for the past few months in the lovely area of Hampstead was, within days, no longer available.

"My new London world, which I've struggled to create, is falling down around me," I confided. "I don't want to go back to Canada where I've spent too many years spinning my wheels, as they say. To make matters worse, I have no idea what I'll do when I get there."

I could feel tears pushing their way into my eyes. What was it about this person that made me want to tell all—or almost all? He was a few years older, but was he wiser?

"I guess I'm a lost soul at this mid-point in my life. Not something to be proud of."

With some degree of self-respect, I spared him the confusing details of my latest unsuccessful relationships—one across the ocean, the other in London itself.

A look of real concern flashed in Chris's pale eyes, as he tapped his wineglass against mine.

"It seems like you could use a little guidance from a life coach about your future," he said with a sympathetic expression. "That would probably make you feel better prepared for 'exile.'"

"I'm open to any advice people can pass my way," I admitted. Was I too whiney? Self-pitying? Neither was a winning tactic on a first "date"—which, of course, this wasn't.

But this was first-impression time; and I was doing everything the experts warn you not to do—complain, sound lost, reveal all. Wasn't I old enough to avoid such relationship pitfalls?

"When you move out of your home in Hampstead, why don't you come and stay at my place by the tracks in Wimbledon?" Chris suggested, completely out of the blue. "I call it the Railway Tracks Hotel," he laughed. "I like to think of it as a refuge where people can adopt new ways of thinking, get on a different track."

"Do you mean a kind of therapy retreat?" I asked, finding it hard to believe his audacity—and my immediate genuine interest.

"Exactly. I have some expertise in Direction-Finding Techniques and so on, and would be more than happy to share it with you. You appear to be an open and honest person."

I thanked him for his kind words while mulling over his refreshingly straightforward invitation. Some practical guidance before dragging myself to Heathrow Airport and beyond *was* tempting.

A timely gift from wherever.

Maybe the universe was "providing"—according to certain increasingly popular theories I'd read about and rather liked. Had my anxious thought vibrations actually summoned this benefactor to me from across the city?

If so, nice work!

"Do you do this sort of thing often?" I asked, trying to conceal my eagerness. "Meet people"—I didn't say women of a certain age—"and invite them to your home within hours? Or do I seem that desperately in need of help?"

"A bit of both, Kathleen."

I soon learned that Chris had years of experience in counselling and what he called "co-counselling"—something I'd never heard of—which involved teaming up with others and sharing problems and solutions. Not the typical, hierarchical therapist-patient relationship. More mutual and equal.

"Would you like some help along the co-counselling line or the traditional approach?" he asked, pushing a wisp of black hair from his forehead. "Either way, I might be able to help."

"I think I would opt for good, old-fashioned counselling," I stated. "Co-counselling sounds interesting, but I'm in the mood to learn rather than share. Does that sound greedy or selfish?"

"No, it sounds determined. Mind you, two weeks is a short period of time and we can't perform miracles, although we can lay some excellent groundwork."

My new pal was probably too optimistic and ambitious, I thought, but I agreed to come and spend the last precious days of my UK stay with him. What did I have to lose? My more sensible self told me he wasn't a total stranger. He had been known and respected at the meeting we had just attended—and I would make further inquiries before the actual move.

I wasn't completely naïve.

To avoid any future misunderstanding, I told Chris a little about the rocky fling I'd been having with one of his countrymen over the past few months—emphasizing that I was still pining. Again, he acted quite neutral, even professional about the matter.

"I think your 'fling,' as you call it, is a result of other factors," he answered mysteriously. "We'll discuss that. By the way, did I mention how comfortable my guest room is? Lots of people have found it very safe and secure during their stay."

He leaned back, as if to give me space. "I know you're wondering what's in this for me. For one thing, I find it very satisfying trying to help people out of their doldrums. And I appreciate engaging company, so I choose my subjects with care. You could say it's my hobby, now that I'm a man of leisure."

His blunt, frank tone reassured me, and helped put any Don Juan worries to rest. I certainly wasn't in the mood to fend off a groping host, chasing me in circles around my bed—even though Chris did have his own charm. I sensed I would be safe with him, and my instinct had a pretty impressive track record.

No doubt, those gentle eyes helped, too!

Also, I reasoned, this arrangement would be better than simply landing at a friend's house—I had other kind invitations—feeling frantic and miserable.

Yes, I was desperate to pull myself together, at least to some extent, rather than boarding a plane to Canada with little in the form of real plans or goals. London had consumed my life and energy in an unforgettable way, as I happily spent a small inheritance from a generous, still-living uncle. But I'd also been in a kind of Never-Never Land. A female Peter Pan, unwilling—or unable—to grow up and accept responsibility for my future until my luck, money, and time had run out.

Not that this had been at odds with my generally meandering, searching route through life! Just more pronounced. Intense.

My six-month escapade had been amazing, but now things had to change—and fast.

As Chris and I continued to chat, something deep inside told me that this was a pivotal moment in my life—and I should take full advantage of his unusual offer.

I might not get another one from him—or the universe.

CHAPTER ONE

There's a Chance

If you don't get lost, there's a chance you may never be found.
—Author unknown

On a cold Sunday evening in February, Chris, who looked dashing in his stylish black winter jacket, came to my beloved flat in Hampstead to collect me and my suitcase. Julian, the man I loved (I'll explain that particular—or, more accurately, peculiar—relationship later), was storing another heavier piece of luggage, which I didn't want to drag around at that point.

It wasn't easy to turn the key for the last time in the door of the cosy old-fashioned place I called home, slip it into the mail slot, and walk through my quiet, pretty neighbourhood, knowing I would return only as an outsider. Those narrow, uneven streets with their cramped front gardens and wayward bushes would no longer be mine.

I had lost my nest, my base of operations.

My life-coach-to-be accompanied me to my favourite local pub, The Flask, for a beer in the glow of a lively fire and some sad goodbyes to the regulars. I had sat among them so often, whiling away cold evenings with great, aimless conversations. We—Grant, the frustrated artist, always in velvet; Colin, the handsome farmer's son, whose much younger eyes I'd avoided, and others—would crowd around a table in the corner, downing our ales as the hours passed.

How painful to put such companionship behind me. But it was off to Wimbledon—my latest destination.

As Chris and I sat in the tube, speeding south underground, I glanced sideways—and up—at him, head and shoulders above me, and suddenly realized what I was doing. I was about to cohabit—in the asexual sense of the word—with an unknown man in an unknown place with unknown consequences!

Was my tendency to be trusting and spontaneous finally going to betray me?

True, my preliminary research into this enigmatic human being had given him an A rating in terms of his public persona. He was considered decent, principled, reliable. Perhaps, though, I imagined wildly, behind closed doors he would transform into a tyrant who expected me to scrub and clean the house for him, run his bath, wash his socks, iron his clothes, and serve him tea five times a day.

Or worse.

The frightening fact was that, although I had insisted on paying my own way in terms of groceries and other expenses, I was going to be totally beholden to Chris for generously putting me up before I left London to start my life all over again.

I felt vulnerable.

❧

Given the annual international spotlight on this community, crowded, dingy Wimbledon Tube Station was not what I had anticipated. Already I missed the one in Hampstead with its bright tiles and amiable attendants. From there, we had to walk several long blocks to get to Chris's small townhouse, a.k.a. the Railway Tracks Hotel—the RTH—with no tennis courts in sight!

So much for the glamour.

As Chris pulled my wheeled suitcase and pointed out local landmarks of interest—not many—the route seemed endless. When we finally reached a small side road, we turned into a cluster of houses that the British call a "close"—apparently, for good reason. We then headed toward a large fence (obviously hiding the tracks and trains) and made our way along a narrow, barely illuminated path to the townhouse door.

My long face was brushing against my kneecaps by the time we arrived. Chris took his key and turned it in the lock. My fate is sealed, I thought, as he opened the door into a gloomy hall, littered with junk mail.

I followed him without uttering a word and found myself in a small, crowded living room, dominated by ceiling-high shelves crammed with books, a computer table covered with papers, and a large recliner chair. There were also CDs scattered around a dated sound system.

It didn't exactly meet my tidiness standards, but then again, some people think I'm fussy.

"Can I get you a whisky?" Chris asked, walking to the tiny kitchen, which opened onto the living area. I nodded with relief. A mind-dulling liquid thrown back with great speed seemed mandatory at that point.

After some light conversation about Chris's own housing history—he had moved to Wimbledon from a large house in Putney after his second marriage failed a few years earlier—he led me upstairs to a guest bedroom with a window overlooking the tracks.

Lucky I wasn't there for marital advice, I sighed, as I carefully pushed aside the curtain and gazed blindly into the thick darkness.

"The noise from the trains is terrible in the summer," he told me. "But it isn't too bad with the windows closed as they are now. I find that it is excellent therapy just to have a sense of movement nearby."

When my new housemate had gone downstairs, I took a long, hot bath in the poky but efficient bathroom and settled into my bed with the music of Schubert wafting up from below. I was too tired to cry, although a few warm tears would have helped a great deal. What had I done this time? I interrogated myself. Why did I keep committing disastrous errors of judgment—not about people, but about me, my real needs?

More important, would I actually be able to learn anything life-transforming in this simple, unpretentious environment with a mystery man?

The next morning, I woke up with a wretched cold. A case of mind over matter, I concluded dismally, staring at the ceiling—my head glued to the pillow.

Psychosomatic or not, it was doing a good job of racking my entire body with incessant coughing, as my congested chest tried to relieve itself. I felt weak and completely unambitious. Hopeless, really.

Of course, I told myself, momentous personal change would be impossible under the circumstances. Deep thinking simply wasn't an option. I would have to bow out gracefully from any counselling plans Chris had for the day.

On the other hand, if my sudden illness were merely psychosomatic, then what? Should I allow my mind to play nasty tricks whenever it wanted—especially when I was scheduled to do something that might turn out to be positive?

I had always been impressed by the power of the unconscious and knew it was quite capable of first-class sabotage. Those stories of people losing their keys when they were about to go somewhere pressing, or getting sick just before a crucial exam had always fascinated me.

I had even heard that the various personalities exhibited by someone with multiple-personality disorder could have contrasting states of health. One could be diabetic, while the other was absolutely fine. If true, that said a lot about mind over matter.

Not being too cruel or sadistic, my mind had modestly settled on the common cold. But why? Wasn't I ready to be remodelled?

Just as I was beginning to feel truly confused and sorry for myself, Chris appeared at the door, holding a glass of hot water with lemon and honey.

"Good morning. Try this," was all he said.

As I drank, the sweet steam circled around my face, and I breathed in deeply. Soon, I felt well enough to agree to a grilled kipper for breakfast—a delicacy I'd avoided since my grandmother had cooked them for my grandfather many years ago, leaving their home smelling like the seashore. (I had almost expected gulls to start circling.)

When I made a half-hearted, "getting up" gesture, Chris insisted on serving me breakfast in bed. "I want you to feel spoiled while you're here," he explained. "You've had a busy, demanding six months, and you're soon heading off to something new. Familiar, but new. It's time to relax while you can."

Agreeing reluctantly, I dropped my head back on the pillow. This humble "hotel" was proving to be a castle in disguise. Who knew? Feeling genuinely grateful, I immediately instructed myself to ignore the papers piled on every flat surface around my room. This wasn't the time to focus on trivial décor details.

There were far more urgent things needing my attention.

─ ✦ ─

After the delicious kipper, which my chef and mentor showed me how to eat safely, avoiding those tiny bones threatening to catch in your throat and kill you, I announced that I was fortified and ready for some introductory therapy.

"I'll get dressed and meet you downstairs," I said with forced gaiety.

"Why don't you spend the day in bed?" Chris asked. "I can take care of you. No problem there. But are you sure you want to get started on the exercises now? Perhaps you should simply take a break."

This led to a diplomatic round of negotiations. With Chris perched at one end of the bed and me under the covers at the other, we discussed the best plan for the day, considering my illness. Eventually, we decided I would stay where I was—and get down to business.

Compromise is always a good thing. The world could use a lot more of it.

Yes, indeed, I was determined that my cold was *not* going to prevent me from following what Chris had so temptingly called his Direction-Finding Techniques—since it was all too clear that my direction badly needed finding! So I decided to reverse the mind-over-matter phenomenon, fight fire with fire, and ignore my probably psychosomatic illness—as well as the fact that I wanted to curl into the fetal position and sleep all day.

Straightening up, I adjusted my back against two plump, down-filled pillows to get comfortable, smoothing out the covers, and wishing I had the time to put on just a wee bit of makeup. Mascara always makes me look—and feel—more wide awake.

Once I was settled, Chris began, "Basically, Direction Finding means delving into yourself through a variety of exercises in order to *really* know who you are, what you think, and where you should be heading. It helps you find the *real* you, if that is, in fact, what you wish to do."

I nodded eagerly, causing my sinuses to protest. He then suggested I write down my **Top Twenty Accomplishments** in life. "Let's get your therapy at the Railway Tracks Hotel off to a positive start. First, we'll spend time trying to clearly establish what constitutes you, and then, based on our findings, decide what you should do next!"

I smiled a watery-eyed smile. That sounded like a fruitful game plan—but Accomplishments? Me? I'd never thought about them, and had certainly not put them down on paper.

The closest I had come to such a personal review was my **résumé**, where I had tried to present a brilliantly rosy professional picture of myself in the hope that prospective employers would offer me a great job with loads of money.

That was more like marketing than self-assessment.

Chris soon left me alone with a blank pad of paper and a pen. In spite of his encouragement, this Direction-Finding business was all very daunting, but it didn't take too long before I wrote, "Accomplishment Number One: I've raised a responsible, balanced, and happy daughter."

Yes, I had dedicated the first years of my adult life to "putting another generation on its feet," as my kipper-cooking grandmother used to call it. My daughter was now on her own with a good job, plans to attend graduate school, and lots of friends—wishing her mother would grow up.

Even though I wasn't proud of that last part, I *was* proud of what I'd achieved parentally. Somehow, someway, I'd passed on a certain amount of wisdom and courage—and my child had become an interesting and interested person. Stable too. Perhaps that was because I had often told her to use me as a negative role model, and she had carefully followed my advice!

"Accomplishment Number Two: I have a healthy relationship with most of my family members." There were gaps here and there, on and off, now and then, but generally things were humming along smoothly—especially when there were a few thousand miles between us.

Over the years, I had fought hard, desensitizing myself to the odd insensitive personal comment or wisecrack that would leap from the mouth of a beloved kin. I'd had a certain amount of success—although there were still some damaging verbal dandies.

They usually hit their target with stinging force.

Bull's eye. Ouch.

Friends, I found, were generally more thoughtful and careful. Considerate. Of course, unlike family members, they could be screened before being allowed any real access to my delicate inner realms—mind, heart, and soul.

"Accomplishment Number Three: I was a loving granddaughter." All four of my grandparents were now gone and I missed that solid element in my life. That anchor. In fact, my only recurring dream involved discovering that my dearly loved maternal grandparents (the kipper eaters) were still alive—and I hadn't seen them for much too long. I would wake up feeling devastated because I had neglected them. Even now, almost two decades after their deaths, I'd give anything to run over to their home for a visit.

Was I writing Accomplishments or regrets? It was time to separate the two, if this exercise was going to produce results. Come on. Glass half-full—or more!

"Four: I managed to get through university in spite of obstacles." When I left home to live in residence in another town, I was miserable. I missed our crowded house and my four younger siblings. I wasn't ready for the big, unknown world. Somehow, the groundwork for being an independent adult hadn't quite been laid properly—and all I could do to compensate was cause trouble and rebel, both academically and socially.

I cut a lot of classes and partied.

Oooops! Back to positive!

"Five: Oddly enough, I have good relationships with the men of my past." That was important. I believed that you should make every effort to like the human beings you once thought you loved. Stay in touch. It was the least you could do! I could never understand people who cut off contact with those they had been truly close to and intimate with.

On the other hand, I'd never gone out with a real monster, someone I had to run from. Perhaps that, too, was an Accomplishment.

"Accomplishment Six: I have written many relevant newspaper columns over the years." For more than a decade, I had been expressing my largely unappreciated opinions on one subject or another—from feminism to free trade—and had been published in several Canadian dailies. My columns hadn't had much of an impact on the world, but they did fill a large scrapbook, stored first in a box in a cupboard and then on my hard drive. They also looked good on my rarely visited website—now that I was modern.

"Seven: I have completed the first draft of a novel." With this, I was beginning to grasp at straws. Like my columns, my novel was filed away, gathering dust upon dust, but I had managed to type three-hundred pages into my computer, complete with a plot and what I considered to be a cast of fascinating characters. It was about an older man who falls in love with a younger, fatherless woman—me. I loved my book. It made me weep as I wrote it.

What a wasted time investment, I moaned to myself, in light of my present virtually homeless predicament.

"How many Accomplishments did you say I should write?" I called to Chris, who was reading in the next bedroom.

"Twenty," he shouted back, much to my distress.

"I'm already slowing down and I haven't reached ten," I whined.

"Most people have trouble," Chris declared along the short hallway between us. "We're not used to being really positive about ourselves. But don't worry. I know you're just being modest. You've had an interesting life from what I've heard so far and have done a lot. Be systematic. Start with your childhood and work from there."

"Childhood? Accomplishments?" I yelped, followed by a sudden sneeze.

Maybe a little exercise might help stimulate my weary brain. Easing myself from my bed as quietly as possible, I tiptoed the few feet over to the window, ready to admire whatever view there would be in the light of day.

Horror of horrors, a train was sitting on the tracks just beyond the fence! It was only yards away from me—and packed with people. Could they see me standing there in my nightie with my hair unbrushed and askew? I ducked quickly, like a gangster in a shootout dodging a hail of bullets, and scurried back to the privacy of my bed.

Where was my Hampstead view of the city? I mourned.

As if that momentary shock had kick-started my mental circuits, I immediately wrote, "Accomplishment Eight: My father adored me." He died when I was five years old. I was his first-born and everyone marvelled at how close we were. I could still remember vividly—and painfully—some of our times together, even though I was so young. He would sing Irish folk songs for me while looking in the mirror, shaving. There was always a touching rendition of "I'll Take You Home Again, Kathleen."

Yes, Daddy had made quite an impression on my fresh, innocent heart. I suppose you might call him my first love—or first lost love. I was still trying to get over him.

Hmmmm . . . Childhood. Child-hood. "Nine: I was the best tree climber in the neighbourhood." In spite of my advancing age, I was still quite skilled at manoeuvring my way from one limb to another. People were always shocked when they saw me, fully grown, balanced on a branch high above them. "Ten: I was good at track and field, especially high jumping." "Eleven: I won a public speaking contest in Grade 4." "Twelve: I wrote several chapters of a novel when I was ten."

The great moments of my young life were falling from the back of my mind onto the paper like pennies from heaven.

"When you've been through your childhood, move on to adolescence," Chris advised from afar—a disembodied voice of encouragement. Somehow, he seemed to be looking over my shoulder.

"No problem!" I shouted happily.

"Thirteen: That English essay on Ibsen's play *A Doll's House*, which the teacher described as intelligent and original." "Fourteen: I was the secretary of the High School Union of Students." It was a modest beginning to my interest in politics, but I was there, standing up for my young rights—involved.

"Fifteen: I was a fashion setter." When the style called for short skirts, I dropped my hemline. When the look was longer, I went mini. I spent hours in vintage clothing stores finding unusual dresses, skirts, suits; I bought over-the-knee, leather boots before they had come to my town. It was entertaining and creative—although I did get a lot of strange looks.

Once, in spite of the address I had given him, a taxi driver delivered me to the local convent, assuming my long grey winter coat was a nun's habit.

Big mistake there!

Chris was right. Looking back at those days was fun—and, very possibly, therapeutic. I began to rush through my various university academic and social Accomplishments. That period hadn't all been bleak. My first Philosophy 101 essay, praised by my professor; the article I wrote for the university newspaper on the restrictive rules governing student behaviour. It caused such a stir among school officials. I think they feared the revolution had begun!

Then there was the day I walked thirty kilometres to raise money for charity. I couldn't walk that evening, but I could certainly dance—once assisted onto the dance floor. Different muscles, it seemed.

Who knew I'd been so busy and even hardworking? It really was astonishing how little I appreciated my own action-packed past.

On to my adult years. I wrote down various jobs and positions I considered Accomplishments: healthy relationships I had established and maintained; places I'd travelled to; little victories I'd achieved.

"Accomplishment Thirty: I helped save the historic courthouse in my community." I'd stood up in front of the city council and delivered a speech in defence of preserving that iconic building where my grandfather and father had practiced law. When I'd finished, audience members were grabbing my hand to shake it, as I took my seat.

Ah, the exhilaration of fighting for something you care about!

Then there was my job with a provincial cabinet minister which had involved speaking to the mayors and citizens of various communities about their problems. I bragged happily that I saved towns for a living. And then . . .

"More hot lemon?" Chris asked. I hadn't heard him leave his room and go downstairs, and now he was standing beside me, cup in hand. What a guy. "I hate to interrupt. You haven't stopped thinking and writing for the past hour. But consider this a work in progress."

"You certainly opened the floodgates," I sighed. "This has been amazing. It's like flying over my life, looking for all the very best things, picking them up, and admiring them. Nothing negative."

Chris laughed a little too heartily. "That comes next! At this point, I'm glad you've managed to find reasons to be proud of yourself. It helps, especially when you are in a state of flux and uncertainty. Now let's have a break. How about a little Chopin to cure that cold?"

He walked over to the small sound system sitting on my dresser and inserted a CD he had brought from his collection in the living room. "This will also get you in the mood for your next task, if you feel up to it."

Slightly worried by his tone, I asked what my second assignment would be. "As long as it doesn't require me to put on regular clothes and look decent, I'm keen," I told him. And I was. I was getting into this self-awareness game and wanted to keep playing.

Also, I knew my time at the RTH was limited and I should take advantage of this day off from my other plan—to see as many London friends as possible before leaving.

"When you're rested, I'd like you to write down your **Top Ten**—no, Seven—**Failures**," Chris said. "Only seven because of your cold. I'm taking pity on you! The point of this exercise isn't to depress you or get you thinking about what you haven't done, or haven't done right. It's designed to help you find new goals and direction. Are you up for it?"

"With unhappy Chopin playing, I think I can come up with dozens and dozens of Failures and disappointments," I said. "He's so good at tearing away at the soul. But I'll be a well-behaved patient and limit my list to an unlucky seven, if that's what you think is best."

"It's what I *know* is best," Chris smiled. "I'm not here to let you wallow in self-criticism. Believe me. That never got anyone anywhere. Once you've finished your list, you'll see the purpose of it. In the meantime, would you mind if I had a look at your many Accomplishments?"

I feigned a look of terror, holding my precious list close to my chest, and then passed it to him. With that, he turned down the music slightly, winked, and left the room. "There's no hurry. I'll be working downstairs now."

Doing what? I wondered. I could picture him going over my Accomplishments with a magnifying glass, analyzing every word, letter, and punctuation mark while consulting the works of Sigmund Freud. What would he—they—conclude? That I was incurably daft—as they say in the UK?

I dropped my head back on the pillows and rested for a short while, trying not to think of my next assignment—which was nothing less than facing the least-productive, least-successful incidents of my past life. This required itemizing the times when I bombed as a human being . . . flunked out.

Talk about a comedown.

Obviously, defining my Failures would take even greater introspection—and honesty—than those many Accomplishments which Chris had managed to pry out of me in his winning way. After all, who really wants to revisit her lowest lows? Wasn't this usually where selective amnesia came in handy? Denial? All those convenient defence mechanisms?

No, I told myself with newfound rigor. It wasn't. Not this time. Not anymore! I was determined to follow Chris's instructions in the hope that he could help me establish a better understanding of myself and find that tantalizingly new direction—whatever it entailed.

London or no London, I had reached a point in my life where I knew I couldn't keep putting out energy without some kind of plan or goal. This meant I couldn't avoid facing my various realities—good and bad—if I was going to change some of them.

I sat up straight, blew my nose, grabbed my pen and paper, and began to scribble. I decided not to think too deeply or try to second-guess myself. I wanted my inner or unconscious mind to do the work for me, to let me know what was brewing in there.

The words that landed on the paper shocked and surprised me. "I didn't keep my father alive." Where did that come from? I had never felt guilty about it in the past—or didn't think I had. Not consciously, anyway.

I looked toward the window and the solid, real world not far from me with those tiny, brick houses in neat rows across the tracks. Sometimes the present, no matter how frustrating or inadequate it might be, was easier to handle than the complicated past.

Being actively engaged in the present, in the moment, was called mindfulness, according to my meditation teachers. I liked that concept—the steadiness of it—and wanted to practise it more often, but the past kept getting in the way, distracting me, tripping me up.

Did I really feel guilty about my father's death? That certainly could explain a few things. My life on the run, for one. Never settling down, never giving myself a sense of security. Never accepting responsibility. Goodness, you never knew what was making you tick!

"Failure Two: I haven't been able to help my mother get over her grief." At least that one made sense and didn't come out of nowhere. My mother was only twenty-five when she was left with three small children after my World War II-veteran father dropped dead on the beach in front of us. I knew my mother had never recovered. Not really. Was there anything I or anyone could have done to help that process? Clearly, it was weighing on my mind.

"Failure Three: I haven't been a reliable older sister." A few years after my father died, my mother remarried, had two other children, and divorced. All four of my younger siblings had needed me, but I hadn't really wanted to take on the role. Yes, a major failure.

"Four: I've been an immature and often thoughtless mother." Like my mother, I was young when my daughter was born and I don't think I was quite ready. If I hadn't been able to handle the responsibilities of an older sister, imagine trying to raise an entirely new human being. Just getting food into that tiny, wiggling, little mouth was a challenge. The twists and turns life presents you along the way can be quite overwhelming.

The rest of my Failures were light in comparison to the first few. "I gave up jobs too quickly." True. I hadn't had a great tolerance for the world of nine-to-five and corporate culture. If things weren't going well, I walked. I remembered saying to someone once, "I came, I saw, I quit."

And, "I haven't developed emotionally re: men." I still didn't know who I wanted or how to find him. My latest relationship in London had been glorious but humiliating. I fell in love with the most difficult man in the entire city—or so it seemed.

Finally, "I can be too self-centred." Oh-oh. Was this obsession with *myself* then and there at the RTH a case in point? Or was trying to improve myself more positive, less narcissistic? I had no idea.

By the time Chris and I got together again, I had had another hot bath, washed my hair, changed into something a little more presentable than my nightie, and descended to the living room.

"Here, sit down and make yourself comfortable," Chris said, pointing to the enormous reclining chair beside him. It did look very welcoming, so I lowered myself into the sprawling thing. Nice. It was almost like a womb, or what you would imagine a womb to be—soft and squishy.

Primal.

Maybe that was why my host and therapist had selected it for his work. I could picture him standing in front of a brand-new recliner in a Wimbledon furniture shop thinking: This should loosen up all those tight-lipped neurotics.

And there I was.

Sitting in a straight-backed chair beside me, Chris began to read my Top Seven Failures silently and seriously. As I watched him out of the corner of my eye, I felt like I was back in school, waiting for my teacher to comment on my latest essay or test result.

That was never pleasant, I recalled, although the level of discomfort depended on the teacher. It could range from excruciatingly nerve-wracking to slightly awkward.

With Chris, it was the latter.

After going over the list a couple of times, while I held my breath, he turned to me with a smile. "As I mentioned, the point of this exercise isn't to wallow in your Failures. In fact, what we want to do now is to convert them from negatives into **Positive Objectives**. Use them to determine what you should do in the future."

He told me that there wasn't much I could do about Failure Number One—not keeping my father alive. That was one of those occurrences in life that simply couldn't be reversed.

"I know the experience must have been mortifying," he said to me in a soft, sympathetic voice. "By that, I mean the true sense of the word—something inside you must have died. But there's nothing you can do about it, except accept the fact that this tragedy is part of you, part of your fabric, and move on."

Failure Number Two about not helping my mother deal with the grief she'd felt for decades over my father's death had more potential.

"You need to turn this from a Failure into a plan of action," Chris told me. "You'll have an excellent opportunity when you go back to Canada and see your mother again. I'll give you more advice about how to do this over the next few days, but for now, would you mind writing down your Positive Objective in relation to this Failure?"

I winced, knowing that I didn't want to return home just yet and deal with what was an ancient family matter. But it was obviously a problem I couldn't and shouldn't avoid—and had been for too long. It was time to face my internal music. So as instructed, I turned this Failure into an Objective and wrote down, "I will do all I can to help my mother deal with her grief."

The same applied to all my past failings. They were springboards for change. "I will be a more reliable older sister. I will be a more mature and thoughtful mother. I will try to hold down whatever jobs I have in the future. I will be emotionally developed in my relationships with men (whatever that meant). I will be less self-centred, more empathetic."

Crikey (another Brit-ism)! It was an ambitious list, but I did like the idea of converting things I was feeling guilty about into things I could look forward to working on and improving. This method didn't exactly wipe the slate of Failures clean, but it did show that they weren't carved in stone. They were pliable materials to be moulded into something useful.

I could sculpt my way to relative fulfillment.

"Now for your Accomplishments," Chris announced, picking up my long list from the small table between us. "I've been studying them, trying to find trends that might give you a sense of where your greatest interests and talents lie. This isn't quite like reading tea leaves, but it does help envision your potential future."

"I've never been big on tea-leaf reading," I confessed, "but I'm ready to hear what you've divined from my list. It seemed pretty chaotic, as I was writing it, so if you can make some sense of the final result, please do!"

"Well, I see that you love to communicate, whether giving speeches in public school or writing essays or novels. That's an aspect you can't ignore when plotting your future and finding a new direction. Also, you've always been active in politics—in the student union or working for a cabinet minister. Again, something to take into consideration.

"Finally, at least for now, you like people, as you acknowledged when we first met. You're a social creature and should work in a welcoming, dynamic environment whenever possible. There are other things, such as travel, but I think we've identified the three key elements in—well, in you. We'll verify these with other exercises, but this is what we've got so far."

"Goodness," I said, resting my head on the pillowed back of the recliner. Yes, I felt that comfortable. "I think you're right. There have always been patterns, although I've never really grasped them. No wonder I've been running around in circles like a chicken with her head cut off. I've been too busy flapping my wings and bumping into things to see the obvious."

"It's very easy for human beings trying to live their lives from day to day to ignore or miss the big picture," Chris said. "That's why we have to take time, stop flapping, step back, and take a good look—as often as possible."

"Preferably at the RTH," I added like a true cheerleader, while holding back the desire to perform a cartwheel then and there.

"Speaking of which," Chris smiled, "it's time for dinner. If you haven't already had your fill of marine life, how about a filet of sole?"

CHAPTER TWO

Where You Go

❦

No matter where you go, there you are.
—Confucius

What long and winding road had led me to the Railway Tracks Hotel? It was certainly one less travelled—and bumpy. In retrospect, perhaps my landing there desperately in need of advice and guidance wasn't all that surprising. I had been heading in that direction for quite a while. It just took time for all the elements of my jumbled life to converge.

To begin with, I had come to the UK after bolting from a version of those all-too-frequent mismatched relationships—with the nicest man in the world. Being with someone kind, considerate, generous, and sexy isn't the worst fate known to humankind; but Ted and I had little in common.

He was a crush from my childhood. In that fragile period just after the destabilizing perils of puberty, I had *ached* for him. He was the guy up the street in the pleasant town of Kingston, Ontario, who drove past my house every night on his customized Triumph motorcycle—his long wavy brown hair blowin' in the wind. He also played lead guitar in the top local rock band, the Varmits, standing on stage looking dreamy.

I yearned and fantasized like any vulnerable groupie.

I was also proactive. Every evening after dinner, I propped myself somewhere in our front yard, pretending to care about flowers and landscaping while waiting for the sound of his chopper. When Ted finally roared by at top speed, I was probably a mere blur holding a rake, grinning hopefully from ear to ear.

Once, he actually stopped to check out the ever-present lawn ornament he had been passing nightly, but my shyness and blatantly virginal status caused him to ride on after a few minutes of extremely forced conversation. I was crushed.

Decades later, when I was in the full bloom of adulthood, Ted finally examined me at a more leisurely pace. But by that time, I was no longer the same sweet young thing. I had been living in larger cities with varied, stimulating cultures—and the exposure to civilization and sophistication had convinced me that there was a lot to learn and enjoy beyond the confines of my adorable birthplace.

This revelation included an awareness of the wide variety of males populating the world. My taste in men—along with the kind of life I wanted to lead with a partner—had changed radically

※

The fateful reunion between Ted and me occurred one summer while I was visiting my mother back home. Like the thoughtful daughter I tried to be, I showed up reasonably regularly, even though I usually felt like a bird being pushed oh-so-gently back into its cage.

One night, I found myself at a cottage party on a quiet lake north of Kingston, sitting around a dancing campfire with too much alcohol in my bloodstream. When someone mentioned Ted and his recent divorce after an impressively long marriage, I piped up, "Oh, God, I had such a mad crush on him once."

There must have been spies lurking in the woods that night because two days later a highly unexpected message was left on my mother's answering machine. It was from Ted. In a very appealing voice, he said he was playing in a rock band again after years of working and being a breadwinner. Would I like to come to the hotel bar where he would be performing on the following Saturday night?

I couldn't resist! Yes, I'll be there, I told him when I called back. Our first conversation in decades.

Walking into that bar, which I knew so well from my youth, was one of those tingly happenings in life—full of delicious anticipation. Each and every waking moment with that level of intensity should be savoured and never forgotten. Kept for rainy days.

What would Ted look like? What would he think of me? I wondered nervously, as my eyes scanned the five seasoned rockers singing and playing on stage. I was decked out in a dress that resembled the one Reese Witherspoon wore in *Legally Blonde*—pink and clinging. It worked like a charm. In retrospect, it probably worked too well.

My first crush and I soon became an item and maintained that status for more than four years.

During this time, Ted was determined to make "us" work. I, on the other hand, was too often wondering how I had managed to exchange my wide, open, worldlier life for my relatively narrow, hometown relationship—sweet though it was.

It seemed I was back forever in that cage.

Six months before arriving at the Railway Tracks Hotel, I told Ted that I needed to get away. We hadn't been having many laughs together for a while—ever since reality had set in with all the discomfort that usually entails. He knew that I hungered for exotic worlds to conquer, and I knew that he wasn't all that interested in conquering them.

Not a good recipe for compatibility.

So early one September, I informed my friend Jennifer in London that I would be more than happy to look after her flat while she was out of the country visiting her sick father for two months. And, after long tearful conversations with Ted, I got on a plane—one of this particular gypsy's favourite places to be, in spite of the limited leg room.

Hours later, dragging my overstuffed suitcases behind me, I took the cheaper non-express train from Gatwick Airport to the Victoria Underground, made my way to Archway Station, and finally hopped a bus up the hill to the charming village of Highgate in North London.

Soon I was floating around a roomy, one-bedroom flat overlooking the city. For a couple of hours, I simply sat in front of the large, living-room picture window, wondering how the heck I had ended up in this stunning haven—how I'd managed to escape.

I knew two people in the Greater London area, but that was it. I knew the city vaguely. No matter! I wanted to make the most of my two months, so I hit the sidewalks running.

First, I decided to use this excellent opportunity to broaden the subject matter of those columns I had been writing over the years. Before I was fully unpacked, I saw a newspaper headline about a Borough of Chelsea and Kensington study on the survival of small independent shops on the fashionable King's Road. Great topic! I checked with a few shop owners for their reactions. I also called the Borough itself for more information on the study.

Yes, I was a journalist in London and it was thrilling.

I was thinking positively and acting decisively—even though I had to admit that I missed having Ted's warmth and immediate support. He had always been adept at propping me up, which I seemed to need all too often. To a certain extent, he was still with me via the Internet—providing a virtual net under my latest tightrope.

Fortunately, he hadn't condemned and abandoned me because of my wanderlust. He understood that I had dreams he couldn't quite relate to and agreed, reluctantly, that I should pursue them—although he would be waiting for me to wing my way back once my curiosity was satisfied.

Nice guys like Ted can be amazingly understanding, which is good news for unpredictable—or just plain muddled—women like me. Sadly, it can be bad news for them.

Finding myself alone for the first time in years, I quickly turned to the only Britons I knew. I phoned my city acquaintance, Roy, an older man I'd met at a conference in Toronto, and went with him to a few films and concerts. We always enjoyed each others' company, but as luck would have it, he was about to move to Brazil!

I also called my long-time Canadian pal, Lori, who lived in the village of Hampton Hill, a southwestern suburb of London, with her two children and a relatively new Irish partner. She was delighted to hear from me—someone who could swap back-home stories.

It would be comforting to have a family to visit when I wanted to.

My friends—all two of them—had busy lives and schedules and I realized I had to diversify. Fast. I started going to meetings on relevant issues like climate change, organic farming, social justice, and yes, war and peace. I also found a cutting-edge venue for journalists, the Frontline Club, that featured films and discussions on the news of the day. And great debates.

These activities helped me connect with like-minded souls around the city, which led to other activities and other souls, which led ... I'm sure you get the picture. On one hand, it was all delightfully eclectic. On the other, I was completely—and typically—unfocused and scattered.

That's how it works when you are chasing something you haven't quite defined yet.

On a literary note, I attended famous-author readings now that I was in a major urban centre featuring such things. At one event in the National Portrait Gallery, a good-looking poet read excerpts from his first full-length book—the story of his parents and youth—to a predominantly female audience.

He was wonderfully thoughtful and sincere. So British and refined. I and the other women in the crowd were enthralled. So intellectual and wise. Erudite, even. As he talked lovingly about his father, mother, and university-age children, we females collectively drooled.

At a wine and cheese reception after the reading, I found myself chatting with this literary genius. Suddenly, a very young woman, possibly three decades younger, came up and tapped him on the shoulder. He excused himself, whispered in her ear, and turned back to me.

"Was that your daughter?" I asked innocently.

He hesitated. "No, she's my partner."

May-December had been outdone by February-December! My surprise must have been impossible to miss or misunderstand. The cultured god looked down at me and shrugged his broad shoulders, adding, "Life is complex."

Complex, indeed. Feeling I had put my big, fat, not-so-literary, foreign foot in my mouth, I mumbled something about looking for the loo and marched quickly away. Was I in over my naïve head, I wondered, the artless girl from the colonies trying to hit the big time?

That incident was balanced nicely by another, more pleasant one at a prestigious reception sponsored by Waterstone's bookshops. After someone pointed out Princess Margaret's former flamboyant husband, Lord Snowdon, I daringly stood in his path as he was leaving—and introduced myself. (An anecdote for the older relatives.) Snowdon didn't utter a word. He simply gave me a kiss on the cheek!

During those whimsical times, I met an amiable couple who suggested I join them at a certain spiritual centre on the following Tuesday for a free, forty-five-minute session of meditation. Typically, I jumped at the chance.

I hadn't seriously tried to meditate since I was sixteen. Then, I had pushed aside the shoes in my cupboard, laid out a small fluffy rug, sat down cross-legged, and closed the door tightly—hoping to journey deep within, in spite of the dresses draped over my shoulders.

Inconvenient though it was, this cramped box offered the only quiet place in my jam-packed family home. Needless to say, after a few unventilated attempts, as I wriggled around restlessly, I decided the cupboard floor was better for shoes, not spiritual enlightenment.

Years later, there I was, sitting on a rigid chair in a large, bright room in Islington, North London, listening to the meditation leader give us a few short instructions—and send us all into the intimidating realm of group silence.

Forty-five minutes of nothing in a crowded "ashram" isn't easy, but I made myself as comfortable as possible, clasped my hands together on my lap in order to let the energy circulate, and tried to clear my mind of all the usual chaotic thoughts—"frisky puppies," our leader called them.

Although I was basically happy with my dynamic new life in London, I wanted to become more grounded, aware, and serene. The idea of controlling what went on in my restless brain wasn't a bad one either. "Lie down, puppies!" I repeated silently.

When the meditation period was over, the leader quietly asked if anyone had any questions, and I put up my hand. "What were we supposed to experience?" I asked, as the couple who'd invited me smiled indulgently.

"What *did* you experience?" he responded kindly.

I told him that I had tried to clear and quiet my mind as much as possible and, after some struggle, had the sense that there was a designated empty space inside my head. Then, every time my mind attempted to wander—or the puppies started leaping about—I would dragoon (great word) it back to that space.

"Very good," the leader said, nodding his head earnestly. "Excellent." I got the impression he was giving me top marks for mind-clearing.

I went to the meditation centre as often as possible but soon realized that it was run by some kind of guru whose style, when I heard him give a talk, didn't appeal to me. For one thing, I didn't like his beautifully cut, Giorgio Armani–like suit and his flawlessly coifed hair. (Was I being superficial? Surely you could be spiritual and well-groomed.)

Besides, all I wanted to do was meditate, go quietly within myself, absorb the calm of the present, and gather my forces. I hadn't come to London to join any group, movement, or cult that would restrict or control me. I liked my brand-new freedom—external and internal—much too much!

Instead, I met Fiona, someone I thought was a kindred spirit, who suggested we go "guru shopping" elsewhere. This turned out to be both enlightening and fun. Once, we found ourselves with about five-hundred others in a cavernous old church listening to a grizzled old yogi.

He sat on a loveseat and advised us gently that although we weren't able to fully control our five senses, our impressions of the external world, we *could* control our internal world—and we might as well make that world as pleasant as possible. Good suggestion, I thought grumpily, if it weren't so difficult to manage.

At the London Oratory, another tiny man with long greying locks and very little clothing led the audience in a lengthy meditation to the beautiful accompaniment of a sitar. Everything was fine until he asked us to line up in front of him, so he could carefully apply a small white spot in the centre of our foreheads.

I rather enjoyed the whole communion-like ritual—until Fiona told me I now had cow-dung ash on my face. Blushing (around my spot), I realized that the road to serenity and self-discovery wasn't an easy or direct one!

My non-spiritual, social life improved big time while I was walking through the historic financial district—known rather confusingly as the City of London—one sunny day.

I had been interviewing a woman from the Financial Services Authority, whom I'd met at a small party. The interview had turned into a gab session about life and love, as female tête-à-têtes sometimes do, until she had to dash to her office for a meeting.

(Little did I know that the FSA, a respected stock-market-regulating body, would soon be constantly in the media after the "credit crunch." So much for my journalist nose for news.)

Because the city was gleaming in the bright fall light, I decided to take my time going home. Being a stranger in a strange land, I had lots of that normally precious commodity. No employment pressures for this rambler!

As I rounded the corner in front of an attractive building, I heard a voice from a couple of steps above me say, "Hello."

"Hello," I said back, before actually focusing on the person. When I did, I saw the handsome, ruddy face of a man in his mid-sixties.

"You look like a sweet girl," he added.

"I *am* sweet," I returned without thinking. "I'm Canadian." There was my inner toddler emerging again.

"Then come and have a drink with me and my mate," he said, smiling and opening the door of a very chi-chi bar in what had once been a prestigious bank.

Oh, why not, I said to myself. Live for the moment—especially in what appeared to be safe and cushy surroundings. Besides, the alternative of wandering around alone wasn't exactly irresistible.

That was the beginning of my friendship with Bill, a self-proclaimed City Boy, former rugby player, great dancer, and all-round ball of energy. Needless to say, he was married—as is too often the case—and this imposed restrictions on our relationship.

Years ago, after the pummelling, catatonia-inducing meltdown of a marvellous romp with a married man, I had developed a strict policy of staying clear of the blighters. I announced to my women friends that, as far as I was concerned, all "taken" males had a highly contagious, deadly disease and should be quarantined. I would no longer voluntarily go near them!

Somehow, Bill and I managed to work around my spouse aversion. We met once a week for a few glasses of wine, the odd dance where feasible, and a lot of happy talk. I gave him a break from his usual schedule, and he provided me with one more pal in a virtually unknown world. We had little in common, since he was a conservative banker and I was what you might call a progressive humanist (I still haven't got a label for myself), but we found each other stimulating.

And I soon learned that behind those expensive business suits with the carefully selected ties lay a thoughtful, even sensitive bloke. Not often the case.

Rich, dynamic London provided me with other fortuitous encounters. One day while I was familiarizing myself with the joys of the National Gallery, which sits solidly facing Trafalgar Square with Big Ben in the distance, I started chatting with a rather elegant woman in front of a large painting known, because of its former home, as "The Rokeby Venus." She looked to be in her early seventies—the woman, not Venus—with permed, silver hair, pearls, and wearing a rose woollen suit.

She introduced herself as Simone.

The mesmerizing painting that caught our attention was a study of the Goddess of Love by Spanish painter Diego Velázquez, looking at her reflection in a mirror. (Don't let me fool you. I am not an art expert by any means, but when in London, I found it impossible not to make an effort.)

Simone and I stood for quite some time in front of the very nude Venus, animatedly discussing the angle of the goddess's reflection in relation to her face. Simone insisted it wasn't realistic. It didn't line up properly, she explained with such certainty that I, twisting my head this way and that, was soon convinced. The artist had got it slightly wrong.

We then wandered through a series of rooms, sharing our likes and dislikes, and soon realized we had a lot in common, in spite of our differences in age and nationality. To put it simply, we both wanted to soak up every bit of culture around us. It was like unearthing an enthusiastic aunt to discover things with!

That first meeting led to our agreeing to make regular future pilgrimages to the National Gallery or elsewhere—wherever our moods took us. It was the perfect basis for a friendship. Simone lived with her retired husband in Southampton on the English Channel and made only one trip a week to the big city, but that was just fine. These cultural get-togethers turned into an indispensable part of my London life—my regular doses of Simone, her wisdom, and lots and lots of art.

After a while, we expanded into furniture and ceramics by viewing the Wallace Collection, located in Hertford House, Manchester Square, not far from Oxford Street, as well as exhibits at the British or Victoria and Albert museums.

We were both delighted and relieved at how compatible we were—always a joyous revelation—sharing an insatiable appetite for each and every morsel of information we could glean from our various forays. Standing endlessly in front of a painting, statue, table, lamp, or whatever, we would point out and discuss this exquisite detail or that. Look here! Oh, yes!

Not surprisingly, at closing time we were always the last to leave. Security guards had to scurry us out, although they were very respectful of the more senior Simone in the process. Little did they know how much vim and vigour she possessed.

I loved my new life even though its spontaneity and variety required a lot more maintenance than lolling about comfortably in my hometown, going out with family and friends to familiar places and events, or watching DVDs curled up on the couch with Ted.

Financially, of course, it was a nightmare to be living in one of the most expensive cities in the world—despite the fact that I wasn't paying rent. So far, the whole fantasy had been financed by the money my wealthy uncle had decided to distribute in varying amounts to family members, depending on their "relative" status.

He had written each of us a light-hearted note saying he wanted to share some of his earnings before he died, so we could thank him in person. As a niece, I wasn't at the top of the inheritance chain, but was absolutely thrilled with my modest windfall.

Money is freedom, if you can handle it wisely—which I was definitely trying to do.

Yes, being a freer, more alive me was an uphill climb in some ways, but it was well worth the effort. I was seeing and learning so much. I was soaking up the history and culture of this relatively ancient land around me in the same way a sponge baking on a rock in the Gobi Desert sun would absorb water. Insatiably!

The only downside was that I had no idea where any of this was leading—and I knew that it couldn't last forever.

CHAPTER THREE

In the Middle

In the middle of difficulty lies opportunity.
—Albert Einstein

As the end of my two months in Jennifer's flat was approaching, I began to panic. I didn't want to leave my bright, shiny, totally unexpected world with all the bright, shiny, equally unexpected people in it. I had told Ted (as diplomatically as possible) that if I could stay longer, I would jump at the opportunity. I had no idea how this would be possible on my extremely limited budget but was determined to make it happen.

In the money-making category, I had managed to sell the first article I wrote on the disappearance of London's colourful, locally owned shops along with a few other pieces, including one on the faster Eurostar connection to the continent—which now left from St. Pancras Station instead of Waterloo.

It had been great fun roaming around the enormous, renovated, Victorian-era station, once threatened by the wrecking ball, taking notes and quizzing people on what they thought of the new look. The "world's longest champagne bar" was especially pleasant to report on, but I didn't earn enough from that assignment to buy a ticket to Paris! A couple of glasses of champagne, maybe.

The freelance life wasn't without its complications.

Before a conference entitled Be the Change, after Gandhi's wonderful quote "You must be the change you want to see in the world," I learned that Mick Jagger's gorgeous ex-wife Bianca, now a courageous human rights activist, would be the guest speaker. When the *Toronto Star* said it would like an interview, I managed to get Bianca's phone number and had a nice, long, friendly, off-the-record chat with her.

Yes, this former jet-setter was very accommodating until she insisted on having full say over the final article and photo—which the *Star*, like most papers, refuses to give. I begged her to be more flexible, but got nowhere. The squabble was fascinating, though.

All in all, my semi-star-studded existence was far from secure, especially as homelessness loomed. It was my pal Bill who saved me.

"I have a large two-bedroom flat in Hampstead, which I've just sold," he announced casually one day in one of our favourite meeting spots. He explained that the tenant he had for years was moving out, but because of some legal technicalities, the new owners wouldn't be taking over for at least a couple of months, perhaps more.

Then came the magic words: "Would you like to stay there for a bit?"

I stared, took a sip of my wine spritzer, and stared a little longer. No words were available. I could only stand there and observe the warm welcome feeling of relief winding its way through my body.

Once again, that old universe seemed to have provided for me. First, one free flat and now another. Incredible! Had I been emitting the right kind of positive vibrations, again? If that was the source of my lucky breaks, thank you, sun, planets, Milky Way, and even black holes.

I wanted to get down on my knees and pray to all those quantum physicists who believe in the unity of all things. Instead, I almost collapsed with joy on the floor in front of Bill.

So at the beginning of November, my third month in England, I could now move from Highgate across beautiful Hampstead Heath—almost eight-hundred acres of what was considered London's largest ancient parkland—into Bill's sold apartment. It too, he had told me proudly, overlooked London. I was truly blessed.

By what—I wasn't sure.

I planned to stay in Hampstead as long as I possibly could. When the time came to move out, I schemed devilishly, Bill would have to pry my fingers from the frame of the flat's front door one by one, as I clung madly, hair flying in every direction, screaming, "No, no, I won't go!"

Besides, I found out I would be half a block from former Culture Club singer Boy George, now a friendly, balding, middle-aged man in a track suit—no long blond hair or makeup—whose flat was in a spooky-looking former Victorian mansion. (One day I lingered outside his gate reading the loving fan messages scratched into the walls there. You can imagine my sadness when I learned Boy had been charged with falsely imprisoning a male prostitute.)

The main thing that detracted from that pre-Hampstead period was telling Ted over the phone that I was about to rip up my return ticket, throw the pieces to the wind from Tower Bridge, and stay forever—well, that's not quite what I said. Hearing his unhappy voice made me understand more clearly what I was doing, who I was hurting, and how I was cutting meaningful ties.

Typically, I made my crazy, mixed-up self feel less guilty by noting that life always has ups and downs, good and bad, winners and losers. The point was to enjoy the ups and make the downs bearable, as well as learn from them—even if there might be the odd innocent victim.

The overused euphemism is "collateral damage."

But *was* I learning anything? I asked myself, as I moved from one exploit to another. Was I benefitting from any sort of psychological or emotional progress? Maturing? Developing? Building? Not really.

The chaos was appealing though.

Something divine happened just before I left Highgate. One day, the Wi-Fi access I'd been sharing with my neighbour through our mutual wall wasn't working. Being an Internet junkie—my only serious addiction—I carted my laptop to the nearest local pub.

Many of these traditional establishments had been joining the modern world by providing such conveniences for potential customers like me, even though high-tech didn't seem to match.

I pushed the door open to the dim, haphazardly furnished room and looked around. Because it was early afternoon, the pub was empty except for five men gathered around the bar. On hearing the door squeak, they turned to see who might be entering—and there I was, grasping my computer case looking more than a little out of place.

It didn't take long before one of them, overcome by curiosity, asked if I needed help. When I explained that I was a Canadian journalist hoping to find a Wi-Fi connection in order to do some research, a member of the group boisterously announced that two of their number were journalists—and I was soon standing among them drinking a pint.

It was then that my emotional fate was sealed. As I talked to the journalists, standing to my left, I turned discreetly to look up at the good-looking, sandy-haired man to my right—who happened to be looking down at me. We later called it our "tenth of a second."

Our eyes met (his were hazel), and everything necessary to make life complicated romantically was communicated between us. Wham! Zap! How does it happen? Who knows, but it does—and when it does, it's miraculous, unforgettable. Dangerous.

As luck would have it, that first pub didn't have Wi-Fi, so Julian—recognizing what had happened between us, I'm sure—offered to take me to another one a few blocks away. I never did use my computer that day. Instead, I drank gin and tonics almost by the bucketful with Julian until midnight. We were mutually smitten. There was nothing we could do about it.

For me, he was the cultured, worldly, slightly rumpled man of my dreams—in part, what I had left my own country to find. For him, I was, well, a welcome diversion from the agreeable pattern of Highgate life—and more, even if more wasn't enough in the end.

So began our visits back and forth between flats in Highgate and, after I moved my few things to Bill's place, between Highgate and Hampstead. We commuted by foot across the heath, by bus, or by car in Julian's case, and saw each other as often as possible, which was daily for a while.

Julian, who was gearing down his successful career as an architect, told me he had been single for almost twenty years, since he had left his first and only wife. He was now happily ensconced in bachelorhood which he found came naturally because he had been an only child. He dated a neighbour occasionally but wasn't interested in anything complicated.

Of course, I should have considered myself forewarned by these revelations—or warnings—and made a record-breaking dash for the nearest exit, but he seemed so keen! (How many women have mouthed those regrettable words while licking their wounds?)

Besides, if I had run, I would have missed a lot of joy—along with the anxiety and heartache. In the midst of the emotional turmoil of the next four months, it was sometimes difficult to calculate whether the balance was worth it.

Lively, fun-loving Julian showed me his London, the place he had lived in and adored his entire life. We spent a fair amount of time in Highgate and Hampstead pubs, sitting by open fires, chatting endlessly. Or we would head to the West End and walk along the various vibrant streets he had known so well when he was a younger "lad about town." Areas like Soho, he felt, had lost their former naughty charm now that they had become tourist haunts—and his favourite night club just wasn't what it used to be.

I didn't notice!

We dined in tasteful, non-tourist-ridden restaurants and drank in dark, below-ground wine bars. We also conducted our own "pub crawls," moving from one atmospheric venue that Julian remembered and recommended to another. After several lost hours, we would wind up our outings and head home—in high spirits but bad shape.

My generous lover—knowing my situation, he insisted on paying for everything—also took me to the countryside to see Shaw's Corner, the red brick former retreat of eccentric playwright George Bernard Shaw, with its revolving writer's cabin in the woods, and Chartwell, the hilltop country house where Winston Churchill lived before and after World War II.

We toured old mansions both in and outside London, such as Leighton House and Hatfield House, groping and kissing in out-of-the-way corners. We zigzagged through Green Park and prowled around Buckingham Palace which Julian had never bothered to visit before. In this regal environment, I bought a shower cap for my mother, complete with a royal crest emblazoned across the top. Who could resist such a find?

But there was no place like home—Julian's home. I would go there and spend a day or two. We would take turns cooking dinner, sit up until four in the morning by the blazing living-room fire, and listen to music I had never heard before.

Julian was going through a new music-appreciation phase and introduced me to Henry Purcell, the seventeenth-century English Baroque composer who became an organist at Westminster Abbey in 1676. I fell in love with my new London friend over and over again as he stood by his sound system, having just put on a favourite CD—listening, eyes closed, hands in pockets, with such pleasure to the music he adored.

My Renaissance Man also played the classical guitar and treated me to short concerts whenever I pleaded. Or he would read me poetry. That was when this dignified British male wasn't jumping up on the end of our bed to frighten me as I lay there waiting for him.

Yes, I fell in love several times.

In many, many respects, it really was a dream come true. During the first couple of months of our affair, he was wild about me. His pub friends could see it; I could see it; anyone around us could see it. He touched me sweetly as we leaned against the bar; he held my hand during our walks; he called me every night when we weren't together; he simply gazed at me.

At one point, he even said he wanted to settle down with me. That was when I blinked, fumbled the ball, made my Big Mistake! I panicked. Was I ready to make a commitment to a new person so soon after leaving Ted? Was I prepared to adopt another country forever? Abandon Canada and my family for real?

My friends old and new in London, who had been kept abreast of my involvement, tended to advise caution. More time was needed, they agreed, before such a decision could be made with any certainty.

With my doubts came Julian's caution. He drew back, became tentative—and I lost him. So it seemed. The rest of my stay was spent trying to rebuild his faith in me, hoping we could establish something genuine. I never did succeed. Although we kept seeing each other and the passion remained, it was more restrained.

In the midst of all the joy, I often felt sad and lonely.

~

My fairy-tale life was thoroughly confronted and challenged by reality in early February after Julian took me for a weekend to Nice in the south of France, where he had once had a seaside flat.

There he led us along the walkway by the water's edge, taking pictures of me against a background of blue sky and enormous yachts or wading in the gleaming Mediterranean. We wandered along the shadowy, narrow streets of the old part of the city, smelling the spices and local herbs. We sat on the beach drinking white wine, being served by efficient—and friendly—French waiters.

I will never forget the food we ate in the traditional seafood restaurants, which my sweet man remembered so well and wanted to share with me. Snails, wild mushrooms, sauces. I couldn't have been happier. (Well, I could have, if we had actually been a couple.)

Then it happened. As we came through customs on our return, the UK immigration officer looked at my passport, noted my various arrival and departure stamps, and reminded me in no uncertain terms that my six-month limit had almost come to an end.

"Are you sure she can't simply stay?" I heard Julian's voice behind me. "She's a Canadian, part of the Commonwealth. Surely she's one of us."

"Sorry," said the official. "That was true years ago, but times have changed. We're EU now."

I could feel Julian's body tensing up. "How long does she have? I do hope you're not putting her on the next plane home—in leg irons."

The official laughed (one thing I like about the British is their sense of the absurd). "You can enjoy her company for a short while longer, but don't get too used to having her around."

No amount of begging or cajoling worked. The officer even wrote the date of my required exit—just weeks away—in my passport. There was no dodging that bullet. It was coming right at me.

"Thank you for trying, Julian," I said as we walked onto the plane bound for London. "You know I don't want to go."

He reached out and gently touched my arm. "I guess I shouldn't have fallen for someone who had an expiry date."

Right there in the midst of the usual boarding chaos, I wanted to grab him around the neck and beg him to marry me, make me legitimate, but I knew him well enough. My divorced wolf had retreated back into his lair and didn't want another permanent mate—at least, not this one.

That was the beginning of the general disintegration of my London life. Days later, Bill informed me unhappily that the new buyers would be taking over my—his—flat two weeks before my being tossed out of the country. I would have to pack up and go.

Julian was more torn than ever and insisted we pull back from each other, get together less frequently. Emotionally exhausted, I was beginning to feel the same sense of uncertainty about us—which didn't help in my struggle to keep him.

But what was there to be uncertain about? It was all horribly obvious. The writing was in very bold letters on the wall. The end—the abyss—was near, as clear as the date written in my passport.

It was at this low point that I met Chris, another saviour served up with perfect timing by whatever hidden powers affect our lives.

So there I was at the Railway Tracks Hotel, more than a little worse for wear. Ready to make up for past errors and ineptitudes; ready for change—not simply for its own sake, which I was an expert at, but real fundamental change in my basic outlook and approach to life.

I had finally realized that it was all well and good to be carefree, but I verged on the careless—and that wasn't good enough for the long haul.

CHAPTER FOUR

Why Not Wake Up?

*You have slept for millions and millions of years.
Why not wake up this morning?*

—Kabir

"A Life Coach works with people to help them grow, develop, and achieve success," my own personal coach explained after breakfast on the second morning when, still cold-ridden, I asked him to elaborate further on what he did.

I had bunked in at the RTH out of desperation, which must be very clear by now, but was becoming a little nervous. Even after Chris had helped me identify my surprisingly plentiful accomplishments and had miraculously converted my failures into Positive Objectives, I was still wondering if I had made the right decision to accept his odd offer.

After all, I still wasn't clear what I had got myself into. What specifically did Direction Finding mean? What would the RTH treatment entail? More important, was I up to the change challenge? Could I face more blank pages and come up with enlightened responses?

Perhaps, I tortured myself silently, I was just me, limited and undisciplined, and no noticeable improvement was possible. Perhaps this whole RTH project was doomed to fail. Perhaps it would be better to accept reality and my not-so-satisfactory status quo—and save everyone the inevitable disappointment.

Less neurotically, I was in an inquisitive mood that morning because it was only natural that I might want to know more about my host, aside from the fact that he was an extremely charming fellow and a talented cook.

(The cremini mushroom omelette he had just served with pride was the fluffiest egg creation I had ever sunk my teeth into—delicious even to my then-substandard taste buds.)

I knew nothing about Chris's counselling background other than what he had told me during our first wine-bar meeting, and that could be summed up by the word "minimal." What actual credentials did he have in the fragile field of remodelling people's lives? There weren't any neatly framed professional degrees hanging on the RTH walls (I'd been doing some low-level snooping), and the people I'd quizzed about him had only superficial knowledge of this aspect of his life.

So far, no one I knew had been RTHed, as I was about to be.

"The relationship is a bit like a sports coach working with someone to help him or her achieve sporting success," Chris continued soothingly, "but a Life Coach helps you make a success of your life."

I nodded as coolly as I could from my familiar perch in the lounge chair, sipped from yet another cup of hot honey and lemon, and tried to divert my attention from my troublesome thoughts by picturing tall, dark Chris as my sports coach, giving orders in a sweat-smelling gym. "Up, twist. Two more. Stretch!" I could also see my middle-aged self in a tight-fitting, brightly coloured outfit, hair tied back, leaping over frighteningly high hurdles or stretching until I seized up and toppled over.

The RTH workout I was embarking on was intellectual and/or psychological and/or emotional, rather than physical, but I was getting the impression it could be just as exhilarating and exhausting. Yes, indeed, in spite of the fact that I had learned a lot the day before, I was beginning to wonder about the rest of my stay.

"A useful analogy is to think of a Life Coach, counsellor, or, in some cases, co-counsellor as a professionally trained friend," Chris explained patiently, unaware of my silly, fitness-club mental images—and my angst. "He or she is someone knowledgeable and reliable who's there for you when needed, ready to give direction and advice when asked."

Those words perked me up. There when needed. Ready to give. I could handle that! I could also accept a professionally trained friend. No problem. Maybe my worries were all for nothing. I really wanted them to be, so that I could throw myself into the RTH battle, the fray, and totally invest my energy.

It took all my strength of will to resist smiling meekly and fluttering my eyelashes gratefully at my professional friend who was sitting in the relatively uncomfortable chair beside me. Even though I still had some doubts, I did feel terribly relieved and protected.

Then I sneezed loudly and broke the magic of the moment.

"Bless you," said Chris. "Are you sure you want to discuss this right now, Kathleen? It's a little on the heavy side."

"Yes, yes," I insisted through a tissue. "Please don't let my sniffles or worse distract you. If you can stand my unhealthy company, I'm eager for anything you want to share with me." Frantic, even. That's why I was there.

"Great. Then I'll show you no mercy!" He began to outline the benefits of working with a Life Coach, some of which we had lightly touched on during our first fateful meeting.

"A coach can help you make connections between and among the scattered bits of knowledge in your head, so that you can understand your own personality: who you are, what skills, strengths, and qualities you possess, and how you wish to develop them," he told me.

"That's a tall order."

"Tall but doable," Chris assured me gently. "Following that, he or she can assist you to establish what direction to take in your life, what you want to be when you grow up, and what you hope to achieve during your lifetime."

"It sounds like you are introducing a person to herself, so she can recognize what she has and do more with it."

"Exactly," Chris answered. "Coaching is about calming a person down, so she has time to appreciate what's inside. It's like taking the cacophony of noises in your head and mind and turning it into sublime music, which you can enjoy and benefit from for the rest of your life."

"What an appealing transformation," I said, seduced by his words. "From cacophony to sublime music. Is it really possible? What if I turn out to be the mental equivalent of tone deaf?"

"I guess we'll find out," Chris responded cryptically.

"Yes, I guess we will," I said, trying not to appear too hopeless.

I shifted in my big, soft throne, put my head back on the small pillow, and prepared to listen as intently as I could. This life-changing stuff was a lot to absorb—and since I had signed on for it, I should calm down, as suggested, and learn as much as possible.

"A Life Coach can also help you identify your core values and standards," Chris continued. Apparently, the quizzical look on my face made him add quickly, "These are the guidelines and principles that enable you to set and follow a defined path in your life—what you stand for; what is important; what grounds your soul while inspiring your spirit."

"That's a poetic way of putting it! *What grounds your soul while inspiring your spirit.* But stand for? I do have certain fairly strong beliefs, although I haven't really defined any kind of life standards."

I detected a slight shrug on Chris's part. "If you want another analogy, the whole process is like mining for the gold and silver deep within you, in your core, along with several semi-precious stones—and making something brilliant out of all these materials.

Something unique and priceless. The real, complete You! I'll explain more about this as we go along."

I sighed with relief. As much as I wanted to know what lay ahead, it did seem best to introduce these new concepts gradually and gently. My poor head was already feeling stuffed up, and I appeared to have the attention span of a two-year-old. (That age *again*.)

"Also, as your coach, I'll be trying to help you increase your ability to learn from any and every encounter—expand your wisdom, if you will. And I hope I'll be able to enhance your capacity to relate to other people, so that you can be a very good mother, daughter, sister, friend, or partner."

"That sounds nice," I murmured wistfully. I liked the idea of learning much more from the adventures life offered, since I had chalked up so many over the past months—and years.

Also, improving my relationships with others could never be a bad thing. I greatly valued the contacts I'd made in London and Before London (BL) and wanted to maintain and broaden them. They were the true riches of existence, really. More than the "stuff" we are constantly pressured to want and buy.

As I was daydreaming about sitting guru-style amid a gathering of happy friends and loved ones, Chris added, "Needless to say, the change process requires work and dedication. Just as it takes time and effort to become a top tennis player, golfer, athlete, it also takes time and effort to become a skilful, wise, and effective human being."

I scowled. Why did everything that meant anything mean work? Could I handle it? "I don't mean to disqualify myself," I said, "but have I mentioned that one of my main traits or character flaws is laziness?"

Chris laughed. "Well, perhaps we'll be able to put that trait or flaw to the test and see if it holds up under RTH pressure."

That seemed like a very diplomatic warning, and I began to wonder anew if it was too late to find another place to stay. Escape, yet again. Could I leap gazelle-like from the recliner, tissues in hand, make a beeline for the front door, and send a friend to pick up my things later?

More to the point, would Chris hand them over—or would he hold them for ransom until I and my defective personality came limping back, begging for another chance?

But I didn't really want to budge. I knew I was already hooked on self-improvement and awareness—for better or for worse.

As if trying to make my situation more palatable, Chris noted that Life—a.k.a. behavioural-change—Coaching had come a long way over the past twenty years. Today's approaches were based on recent developments in a variety of disciplines, including sports, management education, consciousness studies, behavioural sciences, and cognitive research—cognitive being the mental processes we go through to acquire and use knowledge.

"There's now increased understanding of the various ways human beings learn. Behavioural coaches, for example, are able to isolate the appropriate techniques that combine to bring about the most effective conscious and unconscious development."

"Isolate the appropriate techniques that combine to what?" I blurted. "I don't like to admit this, but I think you're losing me."

Chris smiled indulgently. He was obviously used to wading into subjects that were deeper than his listener could handle, and watching her—in my case—sink below the surface as she tried valiantly to follow.

"Appropriate techniques that combine to bring about the most effective conscious and unconscious development. I'll give you an example. Let's take sports again. Timothy Gallwey wrote the classic book *The Inner Game of Tennis* on this subject. He realized that the secret of effective sports coaching comes from managing what's going on inside an athlete's head.

"He recognized that if the athlete's inner voice is relaying negative thoughts and generating negative feelings, she won't have a chance of winning. Instead, she must focus on the positive, which will immediately benefit her game."

My Life Coach made a tennis slash movement with his arm, and my eyes followed the trajectory to the corner of the room.

"Fifteen-Love!" I cried. He bowed, as if thanking me for my support, then it was back to work. No more air tennis, not even in Wimbledon.

"Of course, what has been observed on the tennis courts can be applied elsewhere," he said, "in Life Coaching, counselling, and co-counselling, for example. Often, during 'normal' conversation, much of what's going on inside our heads is a commentary on the other person—and it can be quite negative and nasty."

"Guilty," I interjected.

"A Life Coach can help us change our focus to identifying what is *right* with the other person, rather than what is wrong, or what we *like* about the other person's behaviour, actions, or habits, rather than what we don't like."

Chris sat up a little straighter, ready to make a crucial point. "I've come to the conclusion that the single most fundamental development you can promote in yourself and others is the ability to recognize and analyze what's going well and why, rather than what's going wrong and why. Success rather than failure."

"What a wonderful change that would be!"

"Indeed. This is the issue at the heart of my problem with Freudian psychoanalysis. It's directed at what's wrong and unhealthy with someone instead of what's right and healthy."

I could relate to that, especially when it came to my relationship with dear Julian. Perhaps if I had looked at the good side rather than the bad, the possibilities rather than the obstacles, the outcome might have been different. We could have moved forward together in a constructive way. My heart wouldn't be broken.

Or would it anyway?

"You mentioned conscious and unconscious development. Could you define these two levels of the mind?" I asked, trying to pull myself away from past regrets. "Then there's the subconscious. It's all a little difficult to keep track of."

Chris was ready to answer this too. "For me, the best way to explain these various levels of consciousness is to imagine being in a boat out on the ocean. The conscious mind sees everything at or above water level—the sky, the shoreline, other boats. The unconscious encompasses everything to a distance of about ten feet below—the fish, the weeds—which isn't as visible but *is* accessible and controllable. And the subconscious makes up all the dark, unknown depths below. That's the part regulating our bodily functions and so on which we have no say over."

"I like this analogy," I commented. "I think I can actually remember it and have a real sense of the differences, particularly the unconscious mind, which seems to cause so much trouble. As you say, it's just below the surface but can be oh-so mysterious—and mischievous."

I often felt that my unconscious mind was like a monkey on my back. It kept leaping out, begging for attention, playing tricks, and disappearing. I knew I wasn't in full conscious control of the little beast—but wanted to be.

"It's helpful to have visual aids when you're dealing with these abstract concepts," Chris said. "And yes, that unconscious mind can be a challenge! It contains elements most people think they can't control, such as our attitudes and our emotional reactions. However, we have more power over these just-below-water-level phenomena than we realize.

"Again, Freud claimed that most of our programming was deep in the uncontrollable subconscious mind and this made the modern world feel quite helpless and hopeless. Beyond change. But many people don't agree. They—we—think that much or most of it is in the controllable unconscious mind which can be affected and changed for the better. That's why you're here."

"I love this!" I cried, clapping my hands together. "It's so liberating. We do have some power. We *can* improve. Thank you!"

It was inspiring to think that that monkey could be tamed after all. It might even become a cute little pet on a leash, ready to follow me around and obey orders. Heel. Sit. Lie down. Be quiet!

Those frisky puppies, too.

"Yes, it does free up the mind and soul," Chris agreed. "And you're welcome. I do like an appreciative audience. It may be worth mentioning the superconscious mind as well. This level—in the sky above the boat and water—is the tool that enables us to come to grips with both the conscious mind and the unconscious. If we can train our superconscious to cut in and observe the processes going on in our conscious mind, then we're able to manage it better. We can observe that we are being negative or argumentative and reverse the process by emphasizing our supportive agreeable side."

"You make it sound easy," I said doubtfully. Enthused though I'd become, I was still wondering—and even worrying—about the RTH process I was embarking on. Like a child learning to walk, I needed a fair amount of reassurance and hand-holding, as I made my wobbly way into new territory.

I had visions of falling flat on my face.

"Well, nothing comes without work," said Chris. "I can't deny that, but I think you'll find that the results are well worth the time and effort."

He then outlined **Four Personal Development Strands** which, ideally, we would work on together, although we both knew our time was much too limited. For each Strand, there were activities designed to assist in the development process.

Mental Development: This involved nothing less than acquiring the art of mind control. One aspect involved carrying out an inventory of my cognitive—thinking/learning—skills and identifying which ones needed to be enhanced or expanded.

We would have to make a short list, I suggested wryly. Most of my cognitive skills needed upgrading. Chris ignored my pessimistic interruption. Although it was necessary to deal with all my cognitive abilities eventually, he said, it was best to start with the problem areas first in order to fully come to grips with them.

For example, if I decided that listening was one of the areas I wanted to work on, I should spend time concentrating on the various components of effective listening. More on that later, he promised. I nodded to show I was listening—effectively.

Spiritual Development: Here we would concentrate on my values and standards—those belief systems he had already mentioned that guided my day-to-day actions. We would even be reformulating some of them, so that I would be able to live according to my own self-established principles, not blindly following someone else's.

Being an independent sort, I liked this idea.

Emotional Development: This would involve identifying key emotions, along with the thoughts and thought patterns associated with them. We would then look at ways to manage and control them as positively as possible. Also, we would develop techniques for getting "in touch" with others.

I couldn't wait. This would help me reach my "I will be less self-centred" Positive Objective!

Physical Development: This involved identifying any physical and health related changes needed, with a regime that would help bring them about. Fortunately, one of the most positive features of my life was my good health. I rarely got sick, which meant that my cold was a puzzling and probably very revealing exception.

So Chris and I agreed that this category would mainly entail eating well and continuing to get exercise rushing around the city. Those stairs in and around the underground were a great cardio workout.

It was at this point in our discussion that my co-counselling powers kicked in and I suggested something very basic which would help both my/our Physical and Spiritual Development: deep breathing. I explained—and demonstrated from my lazy perch—the value of inhaling right down into the belly and exhaling so powerfully that the navel almost touched the spine.

This, I told Chris, helped release any stale energy residing deep inside. It was a kind of internal spring or year-round cleaning. He inhaled deeply and indicated his approval with a two thumbs up.

"It's strange how we humans neglect the most basic, health-enhancing activities," he observed after exhaling. "Then we spend a fortune on quick-fix gimmicks that amount to nothing."

A kind of sad silence fell on us. The deep breathing seemed to have released more than stale energy.

"I have to remind you," Chris stated briskly, "that since nothing works perfectly the first time, it's best to repeat most of the RTH development activities at least three times, reviewing what has been accomplished each step of the way, so there's definite improvement as you go along."

He shrugged. "Because you have only limited time at the Railway Tracks Hotel, that's a luxury we can't afford. We'll do our best, though."

"Yes, this has to be a crash course," I grumbled. How frustrating life is, I thought. You find the right situation (my doubts were on hold for now), the possibly perfect person to help solve at least some of life's problems, and then discover that things simply can't be all they have the potential to be—in this case because I had a plane to catch.

It was enough to make me weep. I was so very near an opportunity to learn and change—and yet soon to be so far away once I left the country. We would just have to make the most of what we had, and I would have to stop wasting precious time on fruitless uncertainty!

Chris continued, oblivious to my mood (I hoped), "Before the end of each session, feel free to let me know what development area or issue you'd like to concentrate on next. Try to keep this in mind as we do the exercises, although again, there are time constraints. The entire undertaking should be about what *you* want and need."

"That's great." I smiled, and cringed. (I was such an open book.) "This truly *is* work, isn't it? It's quite serious."

"If you want to accomplish anything before you get on that plane to Canada, you do have to work hard and concentrate on the task at hand. Like everything in life, you get out of it what you put into it."

He reached over to squeeze my arm gently. "I don't mean to sound preachy, but, unfortunately, that's the way things are."

Knowing how much I'd been skimming my way through life, I had to agree. Effort wasn't really my middle name. Many things had come fairly easily, as I grew up. I was a healthy, reasonably attractive, middle-class person. Good things in life had been handed to me.

Now, for some reason, I wanted more. More of what I wasn't sure, but I wanted something new, different, and bigger. Less shallow and superficial. More substantial and focused. Satisfying. That required skills I either didn't have or hadn't developed.

So at this point in my life, the challenge was to grasp and apply those skills as quickly and diligently as possible—which was precisely where Chris and the RTH came in. That was why, even though the whole arrangement in his home by the tracks was highly unusual, I felt I couldn't fight fate.

I needed to be there.

"By the way," Chris added over the muffled sound of a train rumbling past, "all personal information is totally confidential. Nothing you tell me will be passed along to anyone else without your agreement, your permission."

"I'm not overly obsessed with privacy," I told him. "I grew up in a large close family. I used to do my homework on the vanity in the upstairs bathroom because it was the only quiet "desk" in the house, even though there were interruptions. Secrets were a luxury."

"Well, I'm glad you're ready to be open with me. Things will work much more effectively that way. I want you to feel confident that the RTH is sealed tight like a vault. If you do discover anything you want kept secret, this is the place."

We then agreed that I would spend the afternoon relaxing with a good novel I had found in his bookshelf, blowing my nose, and drinking the lemon-and-honey concoctions he promised to keep supplying me with. There was certainly nothing pushy about him, even after what he had just said about working hard. With his touching sensitivity, he had insisted that additional recuperation time was needed and I knew with every sneeze that he was right—especially since I would have to abandon the comforts of the RTH and head to central London to meet a friend.

No matter how I felt, I was committed to socializing while I could.

A few hours later, I put down my novel, changed, and walked to the tube, wishing desperately that I could remain in the secure confines of Chris's townhouse.

Why was my life always pushing and pulling me in conflicting directions? I sulked as I trudged along the sidewalk. Why couldn't I simply concentrate on one thing and take it to its final satisfactory conclusion? Achieve worthwhile results?

Even now, I was spreading myself too thin to make the most of the RTH.

When I met my friend Nick at Holborn Tube Station, I brightened up, but he was horrified to see me coughing and sniffling. "I have to give a day-long workshop on Saturday and absolutely can't catch that cold," he declared with a kind but worried smile. I promised to keep my distance and we headed to a classy hotel bar—where we sat as far apart as possible on opposite sides of a fairly wide table.

Nick, a well-respected journalist, had just written a powerful book, *Flat Earth News*, about his profession, arguing that the standards of journalism had fallen sharply—mainly because of cost-cutting by the large corporations which now own most national and local papers.

He revealed how, in the better old days, reporters had had the luxury to thoroughly investigate a problem or issue. Now they were swamped with assignments and often only had time to reword the many press releases that came their way. Of course, those releases were biased, written by people with not-so-hidden agendas.

(Since then, Nick has taken on the likes of Rupert Murdoch!)

I felt privileged to know this intelligent, hardworking man and knew I would miss such connections when on the other side of the Atlantic. If only their brilliance had rubbed off on me—or I could pack a supply in my suitcase.

Life wasn't quite that easy!

After our far-from-intimate chat in the bar, Nick and I strolled to the large old pub where he had been asked to speak to a group called "The London Skeptics." As we entered the long low space, I was shocked to see about two-hundred people either drinking beer or standing in line to order one.

The rowdy scene made me feel a little skeptical myself! Would it be possible to give a thoughtful speech followed by a serious discussion in such an environment?

Amid the cheery, beery camaraderie, the event organizers led Nick and me to a round table at one end of the room. Nick was asked to stand in front of a makeshift microphone and sound system to deliver his speech, and I was given a seat in the front row a few feet away from him.

Not long after my friend had begun his talk, my skepticism evaporated. The audience had become surprisingly quiet and respectful. Things were going extremely well. And then, I felt a tickle in my throat. I tried swallowing several times to soothe the affected area, but it got worse, more demanding. Excruciatingly so. My eyes began to water.

Frantic, I began to dig around in my purse for a mint to suck on. I often took a couple for such emergencies when they were offered in restaurants. As I poked and prodded in the depths of my bag, I sensed my temperature rising, my armpits tingling.

This could not happen! I was not going to disrupt Nick's speech on the state of the modern media with a loud, uncontrollable coughing fit—especially when I was sitting right under his nose.

Finding nothing in my purse that might qualify for first aid, I realized I had no choice but to make a run for it before I erupted. I leapt up, ploughed my way as politely as possible through the dense crowd, excuse me, excuse me, and out the door. When safely tucked away in the ladies' loo, I coughed to my heart's content, hoping that the walls were thick enough to muffle the sound.

Later, I returned as composed and quietly as possible to hear the end of Nick's talk, and the question and answer session afterward. It was a dynamic discussion. Several skeptics were anxious to have their say on this or that usually relevant issue and expounded passionately. Obviously less skeptical!

In fact, Nick finally had to announce to his audience that he had to leave in order to catch a train—a common occurrence in London where people commute regularly from towns and villages. However, he couldn't escape without a very sincere thank-you speech by the chief skeptic and many handshakes.

Outside the pub, Nick seemed pleased with the event and thanked me for coming along to support him—even in my germ-ridden state. Ready to launch into a full apology, I asked if he had seen me jump up and run from the room while he was speaking.

Unfazed, he gave me a big grin: "Sure I saw you, but I wasn't too concerned. I thought you just needed a booze break!"

Was that the non-serious image I conveyed to all my new London acquaintances? I wondered, as I weakly smiled back. I knew Nick was teasing me, but many a truth really *is* said in jest. This time, in my present, fragile, pre-exile state, I was sure of it.

Heading to the tube station after Nick and I had parted, promising to stay in touch, I told myself that I probably should have stayed at the RTH that evening. There was definitely work to be done.

CHAPTER FIVE

Live the Questions

And the point is, to live everything. Live the questions now.
—Rainer Maria Rilke

It was Wednesday, Day 3, at the Railway Tracks Hotel; and Chris was cooking. Again.

By now, I had realized that those grilled kippers on my first morning were just the teaser. My host loved to cook and wanted nothing more than to sit me down at the table to try another of his spontaneous recipes. I was still salivating at the memory of the sole almandine and his omelette, so I didn't resist or complain—no matter how much noise the big man made banging around in the small kitchen.

I ate and ate and ate with a silly, satisfied grin on my face.

Being a seafood-eating vegetarian—with the odd guilt-ridden return to my carnivore past—the fact that Chris preferred to perform his skills on the wide variety of fish available in the waters around the heavily populated island of Britain was perfect. (I sometimes called myself a veg-sea-tarian and a friend jokingly suggested the term "vegaquarium.")

Sadly, against the backdrop of overfishing and contamination, we knew our fish feasts probably weren't sustainable.

Chris and I had decided during breakfast that a little more housebound convalescence was needed—although because the departure clock was ticking steadily, there simply wasn't time to opt out of other activities for too long. Comfortable as I was at the RTH, I knew I would regret not making the most of my last few days in London to see and be seen by my mainly new friends and acquaintances.

I could already picture myself sitting miserably on the plane, staring out the window at the cute English cottages lining the narrow streets on the ground below, and wishing I'd taken advantage of every single UK second. On the other hand, I didn't want another Nick-like episode, being a bacterial threat to one and all around me, ready to break into fits of coughing at the worst possible moment.

So I had agreed to see reason and stay in all day. Besides, Chris and I had arranged for me to do another development exercise in the evening—and I was eager. I wanted to keep exploring my personality and psyche as much and as long as I could.

It was a strange sensation to be introducing myself to myself. Kathleen, meet Kathleen. Finally. She's a nice person, a little confused, lacking in solid direction, but she has good intentions and I think you might like her.

At least, I hoped so.

I also hoped that I wouldn't somehow come up with a clever way to *avoid* getting to know Kathleen altogether, as I had so many times in the past. There was still a distinct possibility I might conclude that I just didn't want to change—which would be foolish and wrong—or that I would flunk out of Self-Improvement 101.

F for failure.

What would happen then? Where would I go next? My superconscious mind told my conscious mind not to allow my unconscious to worry about such things. It wasn't productive. Stop! Desist! Go to the corner and lie down, unconscious, you troublesome monkey on my back.

So there I was, sprawled in the recliner, waiting for dinner, trying to enjoy the relaxed RTH atmosphere as much as possible with my new chum and counsellor. In spite of the odd disruptive doubt, I felt secure and cared for—more than I had allowed myself to feel the day before.

Progress was being made. Even my cold was slightly better.

But it wasn't strictly lounge time. Chris had asked me to write down my **Top Twenty Skills, Strengths, and Qualities**. This would be similar to writing down my accomplishments, although I soon realized that my SSQs, as Chris called them, were the attributes that lay behind any future accomplishments—if there were to be any.

"Many of us have been taught to ignore or downplay our SSQs," Chris had informed me before heading to the kitchen. "We're told not to show off, or that our talents aren't practical or adequate enough to attain what we hope to attain. But life should be about letting our SSQs shine, living up to our potential. For this reason, we should know these aspects of ourselves as well as possible!"

Like my accomplishments, I had never really thought about my SSQs and certainly hadn't committed them to paper. Once again, the closest I had come was putting together my CV, and that, as I've mentioned, was relatively superficial. Good organizer. Team player. Whatever. Compiling my SSQs required more depth, thought, and purpose.

Chris was fully aware of that, I was sure, but seemed to have forgotten all about me for the moment. I could hear him happily chopping vegetables in the background.

Typically, the blank page was daunting, but I put pen to paper and wrote three headings: "Skills," "Strengths," and "Qualities." I might as well address each categorical challenge in turn, even though I wasn't sure whether I could differentiate one from another with much precision.

Hmmm . . . Was my desire to be organized a Strength? Or a Quality? Was the ability to be organized a Skill? I had the sense that I was beginning to introspect my introspection, if that's possible; I was becoming muddle-headed and frustrated.

Time for a deep breath. Be calm. Collected.

All right. To repeat. My Skills. What were they, actually? I decided to start with the basics—nothing too earth-shattering, just the foundations of my ability to get through a typical, modern day. I could drive, cook, touch-type. What else?

Well, I could speak French quite well, and some Spanish. Hmmm, again . . . Oh, I knew how to read music and play the piano—badly—and I was learning how to play the guitar, and, and . . . oh yes, I was considered a reasonably artistic photographer.

I reached down into my Canadian-ness. I could swim (hadn't sunk yet), canoe, sail with help, and even cast a fishing line quite accurately. I could skate and ski in a wonky sort of way.

Goodness, this was slow going. I could almost declare myself a Skill-Challenged Zone. Then I wrote down "communicator." I did seem to be able to get my thoughts across to others, whether verbally or written. People claimed they loved my storytelling.

What else? Had I no other Skills to offer the world or a future employer—or myself?

Chris stopped chopping. "As I said, these exercises aren't designed to give you a sense of inadequacy," he called to me. "They're simply an opportunity for you to think about yourself and who you are. Don't get tied up in knots."

"I know, I know," I replied plaintively. "But I do feel I've been a bit unambitious over the years and haven't developed many real Skills. I wish I could write down more impressive things. Flying a plane, for example, or scuba diving . . . or even something like basket-weaving. How about skydiving? I know a man in his eighties who jumps from planes regularly. That's when he's not off salsa dancing which I can't do."

"Well, Kathleen, no matter what you can or can't do, you've managed to impress me," Chris said—and began whacking skilfully at something else.

I decided to move on to Strengths. "Willing to self-criticize/change" came to mind first. It seemed appropriate under the circumstances. I knew I was being a fairly good sport, albeit a slightly whiney one, about the RTH challenge. I was managing to fight those niggling uncertainties that continued to pop up.

"Willing to listen and learn." Not only willing but desperate. I was almost at the point where I wanted to rush up to total strangers and beg them to critique me. Please, sir, what do you think of me? I know you don't know me, but how can I improve?

"Adaptable." Able to roll with the punches. (Although I'd often thought that humanity's greatest Strength, being able to adapt to new things, was also its greatest weakness—sometimes adjusting to and accepting the unacceptable. Heavy.)

"Love/like people." I did have a fair amount of social energy, which many commented on and admired. Chris, for one. And what about those stars I'd accosted! "Sense of humour." I loved to laugh. In fact, I've always believed our pressure-packed society doesn't provide enough opportunities for real hilarity—uncontrollable, rolling-on-the-floor, gut-bursting laughter.

There should be more of it in this world.

"Stand up for my principles." I had a fair amount of pride in the fact that I held certain well-maintained beliefs—in a fairer, more just and sustainable world, for example. I only wished I could pull myself together enough to be a really effective activist. Being lost was a waste of time. "Becoming calmer and more *contemplative*." Even during my wild, free, and hectic half year in London, my efforts to bring more spirituality into my life had been semi-successful.

In fact, I was already missing my meditation classes. It was amazing how satisfying being still and calming your mind can be, although I would never forget the class when my stomach kept gurgling after I had had several cups of tea during an incredible tour of the House of

Lords earlier that afternoon. (You *must* drink tea when surrounded by Lords!) I kept opening my eyes slightly and looking around to see if anyone was noticing. Could they tell the sound was coming from me?

Chris was now stirring something vigorously. "You appear to be having more luck," he said loudly over his own noise. "Isn't it gratifying when your powers start to surface?"

"I seem to have more Strengths than Skills," I said dryly. "I'm not quite sure what that means. Perhaps I'm not turning my Strengths into anything substantial."

"Well, we'll look at the list after dinner and see," he responded.

Okay. My Qualities. "Quite generous." I put "quite" because I wasn't the most philanthropic person alive, but I was what they call a "giver"—at least in the London underground where I couldn't resist handing out money to all those musicians. And I tried to be caring and kind to my friends and loved ones. I gave as much as I could—considering my rather bohemian existence.

"Courageous." Yes, this past year had tested my courage more than once. Just being alone in a new city and country was an act of bravery. There was no immediate net under the tightrope. No one really familiar to save me.

"Adventurous." As mentioned, coming to London, knowing almost no one, being prepared to tackle life as it hit me wasn't a bad track record. There was that Canadian "expat" river cruise I attended not long after landing in the UK. Because I got lost (physically, this time), I arrived at the designated wharf on the Thames a few seconds late—and ran down the ramp as the boat was leaving. When someone yelled, "Jump!" I flung myself unceremoniously onto the narrow back ledge—much to the appreciation of those on board.

The organizer gave me free admission.

"Quite sympathetic." Another "quite." I could be a little blind to others' more subtle moods and concerns, but I did sympathize or even empathize with those suffering or in need around me. Perplexed though I was, I couldn't simply ignore the rest of the population and its troubles.

"Committed." I guess this was like the Strength I had written down about "Standing up for my principles." I was consistent and "committed" when it came to being anti-war and pro-planet. During my stay, I had volunteered for the UK Campaign against Climate Change and the Stop the War Coalition. I'd marched in several demonstrations through hectic London. (The best way to see a city is when all the traffic has been halted and you are parading down the middle of the street!)

"Reasonably wise." Time had taught me a lot and I had paid attention to those lessons to a certain extent, although it didn't seem to help me keep my feet on the ground. I was better at advising others.

"I think I forgot to suggest that you write down your Top Twenty SSQs," Chris chuckled, standing in front of me with a handful of knives and forks, ready to set the table. "As before, you got off to a slow start but have managed to get right into it. That's good, but it's time to eat."

"Fine idea," I agreed abstractedly as I pulled myself semi-reluctantly back to the external world—and out of my chair. "It's time to find out what's been going on in the kitchen while I've been trying to find out what's going on in my head."

Chris was right. In spite of my initial hesitation, I had yet again become so immersed in myself that I had lost all track of time and place. Not in the usual way when my mind raced around frantically, worrying about this or that over and over and over, *ad nauseam*. No, it was more directed and productive. Much more.

Feeling quite reassured, I announced: "You know that one of my greatest Skills or Strengths or Qualities is the ability to appreciate your cooking."

"Add that to the top of your list," Chris teased.

We were soon sitting down to a candlelit dinner, centred on an odd-looking fish called skate, which Chris had smothered in a delicious sauce, a beurre noir, dotted with capers. As with the kippers, he had to demonstrate the best way of eating this creature with its wing-like shape.

Could I consider this a new Skill? I asked. Skating of the non-ice variety? (Not a useful one as it turned out. Skate has since been declared endangered.)

<hr>

After we had devoured our dinners and were sitting back in our respective living-room chairs, enjoying our wine, Chris said, "I forgot to tell you that your after-dinner assignment is to write down your **Top Ten Weaknesses**. I repeat, Top Ten only. The point isn't to go flat out and spend the rest of the evening thinking about your more negative side. It's just good to see yourself realistically. A balance."

"Thank you for waiting until I'd finished that tasty meal before giving me such a tough assignment. So it's ten, not seven like my failures, now that I'm on the road to recovery! Actually, my Weaknesses should come easily to mind, unfortunately, since they seem ever-present."

I could feel the foundation of confidence created before dinner disintegrating like a sandcastle struck by the waves of a rising tide. Bit by inevitable bit.

"Please don't think that way," Chris said. "You need to keep in mind that your Skills, Strengths, and Qualities are ever-present as well. We're all a big, interesting mix, and there's nothing we can do except work with what we have and try to improve as much as is humanly possible—which is more than most of us realize."

"I'm trying, I'm trying," I insisted, holding up my wineglass in an awkward kind of toast to myself—and my life coach.

My Top Ten Weaknesses did come frighteningly easily. My pen almost flew across the paper with little thought required. It was like automatic writing! Obviously, my awareness of my Weaknesses was just below the surface, compared to that of my SSQs which was buried under a pile of petrified neglect.

My problem was to choose *which* Weaknesses to write down, since I knew I could only compile a short-list out of the many potential contenders.

"Easily demotivated," "not very tenacious," "too lost," "don't follow through," "not enthusiastic/involved enough," "fear success," "possibly fear commitment," "negatively programmed," "too scattered," "lacking self-respect," "fear more loss."

"Wait a minute, wait a minute," Chris interrupted. He was supposed to have been reading, not monitoring my flight of self-criticism. "I think you've got at least ten or more there. That's plenty. As I said, I don't want you wallowing in your Weaknesses, just recognizing a few of them to get the full picture."

"Well, as you can see, wallowing was easy. These words poured out of me like a negative, psychic rainstorm. Does that indicate anything, any kind of internal malady?"

"It doesn't mean very much," he answered, smiling. "Only that you're too hard on yourself and lack balance in your self-assessment. Like most people, you're letting *you* be dominated by your Weaknesses, not your SSQs. The good news is that your Weaknesses aren't what they seem."

"What else could they be—these ubiquitous demons?"

"Weaknesses are really Strengths that have been mistimed or misapplied. Have you ever heard people complain about how there's a double standard in our society? A woman will be called 'stubborn,' whereas a man is considered 'determined.' She will be labelled 'aggressive,' but he's merely 'assertive.' And so on."

"Yes," I replied. "It's quite revealing. It shows that qualities are often in the eye of the beholder. Society's interpretations can be loaded with prejudices."

"Exactly," said Chris with a sincere look of appreciation, as he reached for my list of Weaknesses. "The same is true with these. It's what I call the **Obstinacity Principle**. What is perceived to be 'obstinacy' in one circumstance will be viewed as 'tenacity' in another. What you currently see as a Weakness or negative is, in fact, a Strength or positive—if it's tied to a clear goal.

"When you say you're 'easily demotivated,'" he continued patiently, "perhaps you should say instead that you require a certain level of stimulation and satisfaction. And if you think you're 'lacking self-respect,' it's probably because you've set yourself quite high standards. Without a defined 'purpose,' you remain stuck in Weakness mode and mentality."

I stared at my companion in amazement. Was it the wine or was he the long-awaited knight in shining armour I was beginning to think he was? Here was this person, this stranger, who was trying to convert all those weapons I had used against myself into crutches—or even tools.

Beating my swords into ploughshares.

And it seemed so easy! All that was required was changing my attitude from negative and self-doubting to positive and self-supporting. It revolutionized the whole picture. But I wasn't completely convinced.

"Surely, this doesn't mean I have no Weaknesses," I said, not very hopefully.

"How should I put this? We all have Weaknesses, but they aren't as powerful as we think. Our Weaknesses are weak, if you will."

"Who put the weak in Weakness?" The wine was making this a particularly hilarious therapy session.

"I know you don't comprehend completely, but the RTH treatment programme is an ongoing process with each exercise reinforcing the last. For now, I simply want to plant certain ideas in your head, so that as we go along they can bubble away in there."

He pointed his finger directly at that spot in the middle of my forehead where the cow-dung ash had been placed by the guru. It seemed to be a popular focal point—the brow energy chakra, I'd been told. The third eye.

"Now," said Chris, "why don't we watch *BBC News*? I'm a little concerned about what's happening beyond our walls. Too much bombing and killing of innocents, I'm afraid."

I looked at him sadly. As I mentioned, we had met during a war and peace discussion group and had later affirmed our mutual disgust with those in power who pushed for violent—and more profitable—solutions to most of the world's problems. We had told each other we wanted to help promote peace both externally and internally.

Now, there we were—totally immersed in my small world and problems. I realized I was taking Chris—and myself—away from more urgent matters.

"That's an excellent idea," I said. "It's time we got back to the real issues of the day. I'm sorry I've been distracting you."

Chris stood up. "If I had my way, I wouldn't look at the news ever again. I'd much rather concern myself with people like you who want to make more of themselves in an honest way, so they can function better in society and help improve things."

He walked toward the small, old-fashioned, far-from-flat screen. "But ignoring the outside world, especially in this time of financial corruption and meltdown, is a luxury I don't think any of us can afford. If we don't participate as knowledgeable citizens, we're letting down our beliefs and principles. And our children. Can't do that."

He turned on the telly and returned to the straight-backed chair as I made myself more comfortable on the recliner. We looked deceptively like a contented couple winding down after a typical workday—which, of course, was far from the case.

For me, at least, it had been another revelation-filled few hours of turning myself inside out. Discovering. Examining. Accepting.

As pictures of international mayhem appeared on the screen, I couldn't take my mind off the RTH. Would Chris and I be able to keep up this therapeutic pace and this uniquely stress-free relationship until I had to board my plane in ten days?

Please make it so, I whispered, to the sound of televised gunfire.

CHAPTER SIX

What Is Possible

Knowledge of what is possible is the beginning of happiness.
—George Santayana

Today was my day with Simone, my gallery/museum companion, and no amount of throat tickles or badly timed sneezes was going to make me miss it.

At the same time, I could tell that Chris didn't want me to avoid the RTH treatment completely. When I told him that Simone and I weren't meeting until noon, he quietly suggested that I do some SSQ and weakness follow-up. "This won't take long. I promise."

It was clear he didn't want to be seen as some kind of psyche tyrant, making impossible demands on my time and energy. So far, he had been anything but—and I tried to make sure that he knew that I knew that.

"You've been the epitome of kindness and generosity," I said. "Not only have you taken me, a stranger with a cold, into your home, but you've led me through these lessons with such patience. This is so *not* therapy boot camp!"

As was our way, we worked out a compromise. I would do a couple of short, but thought-requiring exercises, and then run off with my friend to Kensington Palace—because that was where Simone and I had decided to go for our last outing together.

What a contrast! From the RTH to the palace where Princess Diana had lived with her prince. I liked the range.

Chris asked me to list **Five Occasions When I Felt Really Good About My Actions, Behaviour, or Role**. Naturally, that would require me to dig into my past (not always my favourite place), but scouring my history for times when I felt great about myself shouldn't be too arduous.

He suggested I think about them while in the bath—or bahth, as he pronounced it. "Soaking seems to help thoughts and impressions buried deep within our unconscious rise to the top," he advised as I proceeded to the bahthroom, pen and pad in hand.

He was right. As I lay in the tub, head resting on the hard porcelain, long-forgotten memories and impressions rose to the surface of my grey matter. I remembered making a speech while in public school about the fifteenth-century French heroine Joan of Arc. Standing in front of the class, I felt confident because I had already recited those words at least twenty times to anyone in the family who would listen. Or the mirror.

(Ooops, that was one of my accomplishments. Oh well.)

I could also recall helping my grandmother when she was in the hospital about to have hip surgery. None of the other relatives had been available, so I took full responsibility, making sure she was happy and optimistic when wheeled off to the operating theatre—although I did flinch when she realized she'd forgotten to take out her false teeth and smuggled them to me in a tissue at the last moment.

The same pride applied to the birth of my daughter, which was as natural as possible in a modern-day hospital. I had had to be *very* assertive when the doctors kept insisting on this drug or that, but held my ground. When it was all over and my baby was in my arms, one of the nurses told me how impressed she was that I had had the courage to give birth the way I wanted to—not the intrusive way some of those white-coated men in authority preferred.

I needed two more Felt-Really-Good Occasions. I washed and rinsed my hair, thinking, thinking. The hot water rushing over my head seemed to be helping the process—something to remember the next time I was looking for inspiration—but it didn't help enough.

Two more. I turned the water pressure up for added stimulation. As with my accomplishments, I was shocked at how difficult it was to come up with positive events from my past. Was it me, or did most humans somehow stash life's better souvenirs like pirates burying their illegal booty deep in the sand? And once the positives were nicely out of the way, then insist on accenting the negative?

That's for sure! If Chris had asked me for Five Occasions When I Felt Really Bad About My Actions, Behaviour, or Role, I'd probably have had them written down before I was even in the tub. Oh, oh, be careful what you wish for, I warned myself. He will probably ask for just that!

Back to the Felt-Really-Good Occasions. Well, there was the time I visited the office of a former Canadian prime minister, then still a member of parliament, with a questionnaire for a university course. This eminent man, known for being headstrong, began to lecture me on the survey topic—until I interrupted to tell him that wasn't exactly what I wanted.

He was furious! I was a "rude and abrupt young woman," he declared. He slammed his hand down on his desk, pointed to the door, and ordered me to "get out." Somehow, I coaxed and cajoled him into letting me stay—for an hour—and he even invited me back, although we never did get to my prepared questions.

Wasn't there anything more recent along the lines of Felt Good? What had made me feel warm all over—besides fantastic times with Julian? I suddenly remembered several occasions over the past few months when I had attended lectures on various hot topics of the day. During the audience-participation segments, I'd often asked the speaker or speakers probing questions—and audience members had come up afterward and praised me.

A couple of times I had even received applause. Yes, I really Felt Good about that inquiring, thought-provoking role. Me at my journalistic best.

I stepped out of the tub with a sigh of relief. Somehow, I had dragged a few good, bygone moments kicking and screaming from those dark recesses where my mind and mentality had hidden them away. I suspected that Chris had a theory on why that might be—why the good things were so inaccessible and the bad so right there, front and centre.

Given what I'd learned so far at the RTH, I had a hunch what that theory might be.

❧

Half an hour later, I was in the living room with my latest revelations, wondering what on earth my coach would make of them. Sure enough, he had a plan.

"Now try identifying the reasons why you Felt Really Good in each case," he said, after reading my slightly damp list, "and we'll try to establish what overlooked skills, strengths, or qualities you demonstrated."

As I let my hair dry, I put my brain to work. I decided to wing it. Be spontaneous, unrestricted. Now that I had brought these times to light, I had a fairly good idea why they had surfaced.

"I Felt Really Good about the Joan of Arc speech because I'd worked hard, spoken well, and achieved excellent results—a high grade from the teacher," I told Chris. "And I loved speaking to the class.

"I Felt Good about helping my grandmother because I adored her and liked being able to take control in a difficult situation. Be responsible.

"The same was true with the birth of my daughter. I wasn't afraid to make reasonable demands in the hospital and get what I wanted—again, in a difficult situation. Very difficult. I was moaning and groaning with labour pains while standing up, so to speak, for my rights as a woman to have the kind of birthing experience I wanted.

"And I was proud of standing up to our former prime minister and earning his respect. I guess that was why I really Felt Good about asking probing questions at those lectures. Being respected—a leader in some way."

Hey, I thought, as I breathlessly came to a halt, this is getting easier. I'm beginning to understand what makes me tick.

"So let's try to sum up here," Chris said. "Hard work and getting results. Public speaking. Helping those in need. Standing up to authority. Speaking out on issues. Providing leadership. Does that sound right?"

I nodded. He did have a way of getting to the nub of things.

"Did you know when you woke up this morning that you would be exposing all these good skills, strengths, and qualities about yourself?" Chris asked.

"You've got me again! It's almost impossible to be negative around here. I seem condemned to like myself better!"

Chris shook his head. "Not so fast. I'm afraid I'm going to spoil part of your day by asking you to think about **Five Occasions When You Felt Really Bad About Your Actions, Behaviour, or Role**—when you were ashamed of yourself. You'll have plenty of time while travelling into London. I wouldn't ask otherwise."

"All right, Doctor. I'll plumb the depths before Kensington Palace. Knowing I'm on my way to such a historic site where endless intrigue has occurred could inspire me to think about my own past. Years ago, I might have been beheaded for my behaviour, and I would definitely have Felt Really Bad!"

Soon I was heading out the door with a mild sense of homesickness welling up in my tummy. Chris and the RTH were starting to grow on me. I couldn't remember the last time I had had such a feeling of contentment—both physical and emotional. It wasn't a question of love exactly but respect, appreciation, and trust—good things that were all too rare.

Highgate and Hampstead had been enchanting places to live and play in, but I had been on my own—struggling, unsupported, losing ground in terms of my sense of self. Now I was fed, soothed, and supported the way most human beings should be—but too often weren't.

How lucky I am, I thought as I made my way through the Wimbledon Tube Station crowds, past the women selling flowers, past the Cornish pasty shop with its tempting smells, and through the turnstile with my pre-paid electronic Oyster card.

Once seated on the District Line above-ground train, I tried to ignore the commotion around me and turn inward, deep, deep down. What were Five Occasions when I didn't feel good about myself in the past? Recovering them certainly wouldn't be the most uplifting thing to do. The opposite of soothing.

When it came down to it, did I really want to bring them up to my conscious mind? Of course, it wasn't the best idea to let them stew in my unconscious either. They were there, affecting me in some way. It *was* time to bring them to the surface. Expose and confront them!

As usual, I decided not to think too long and hard about this. I pulled out my trusty paper and pen and wrote down, "I 'pushed' my little sister into the water."

It had been an accident. When I was eight years old, I had pretended to push her off the dock and she'd slipped in. The water wasn't deep and she was wearing a life jacket, but she screamed and screamed. There were plenty of relatives around to save her, but it was quite a scene. Everyone thought I had done it on purpose. Oh, that was horrible. I ran and hid under the bed . . .

I peered around the train car to see if nearby passengers could detect what was going on in my head. It appeared not—so it was back to the past. "I hurt my daughter's father." I had been young and foolish, not knowing who I was or what I wanted. (Sound familiar?) I had been very insensitive with him, very undiplomatic, and had hurt him badly because he'd truly loved me. (Had anything changed? Hadn't I hurt Ted in the same way?) I could still remember the night he begged me to stay . . .

"I left a great boss when he needed me." Again, I let someone down because of my scattered life. A principled, highly respected man had hired me to be his assistant, but I found office life dull and restrictive and soon quit the job. It was difficult to see this dignified man almost weep when I told him I was leaving.

I stared out the window briefly before scribbling, "I have been chasing after a man with no self-respect." Me with no self-respect, not him. Yes, the past few months with Julian had been humiliating. Why had I allowed myself to be treated like that—continually pushed away? I knew Julian's resistance was a reaction to my own initial doubts about a relationship, but once he'd made his position clear, why did I keep going back?

More to the point, why did I put myself in that compromising position in the first place? With a man who had warned me he wasn't exactly committed to . . . committing; who would shy away at the first opportunity. What was missing in my value system—if that was indeed the problem?

I hesitated as fretful questions rushed through me.

Didn't I think I deserved real love? Was that why I ran from Ted? Perhaps I was a female Julian. Quite possibly. Where did that leave me?

Related to this, I Felt Bad because "I haven't been clever and resourceful enough in London." I'd made lots of friends but hadn't managed to secure myself anything solid or permanent—personally or professionally. Typical.

I slumped down in my seat. Some of these Felt-Really-Bad Occasions seemed awfully close to failures, but I realized that the point was to dredge all these concealed or semi-concealed negative aspects up in one exercise or another. Draw them out from wherever they were lurking.

In spite of the fact that the now-underground train car was filling up as we neared London, I put down my pen and closed my eyes. In one way, I was glad that my Felt-Bad moments weren't horrendous. Painful and demoralizing, indeed, but not horrendous. I didn't have to regret having injured or murdered someone. I had never stolen or robbed.

Cheering myself up, I recalled the time in my pre-teens when some older friends and I walked barefoot into a Woolworths store where we each casually put on a pair of flip-flops and walked out quickly. Suddenly, I felt guilty and, flip-flopping noisily, ran back inside to return my pair. The older girls were furious because my last-minute burst of conscience might have exposed them as they stood on the sidewalk wearing their ill-gotten goods.

Yes, my Felt-Really-Bad moments weren't anything to go to court over. They were the often-insensitive, sometimes-cruel acts of a mixed-up character. As I stepped off the District Line and manoeuvred back to the earth's surface on one of the long, steep escalators, I wondered what Chris would say about them later that night.

In the meantime, it was five minutes to twelve and Simone and I had arranged to meet at the Kensington High Street Station at noon. I was needed in the present time. The past—at least, my troubled past—would have to wait.

Simone was there. She was always there—on time and with a smile, even though she had to come all the way from Southampton. As I approached, I realized that she looked like one of the most benign people on earth—silver necklace, tasteful jacket, and well-below-the-knee skirt. Few would think that she was a classical pianist who had once thrilled audiences in far-away countries, or that her husband was one of the first climatologists to caution about global warming—decades ago.

Because of this, our lunches and teas together were filled with conversations about the renowned concert halls of the world, and the struggles scientists were having in warning the planet about the dire consequences of the climate crisis. I felt I'd been thrust onto the international stage in more ways than one.

Yes, I was lucky to have found the consummate friend and fellow art and history lover in this big city. Simone was made to order as she tried to expand her own life beyond the piano. A great companion with no strings attached. (Unplanned pun!)

Many would say that the universe had provided very generously, again, responding to my wish for someone who would help broaden my London horizons. It certainly seemed that way—but I wasn't going to question my luck too thoroughly.

"First, I want to take you for a farewell lunch," Simone announced as we walked out of the station to the fashionable Kensington High Street. "There's a little French bistro around the corner you will like."

We walked along the street with its high-end chain stores, craning our necks to look above the ground-floor commercialism at the fascinating details on the upper storeys. As Simone and I had slowly extended our appreciation of art to furnishings and interior decoration, we had also begun timidly to include architecture. We would spend hours staring at the intricate facades of buildings around the city.

It was all a little overwhelming because we knew so little about the subject, but what a feast for our eyes! Intricate brickwork, gargoyles, buttresses—flying or otherwise.

During lunch, Simone pulled a couple of parcels from her carryall. "I can't let you leave without some things to remember our time by," she said, pushing them gently in my direction.

I could feel myself becoming sentimental even before I had carefully removed the neat wrapping paper. The first gift was a soft, sheer Monet scarf from the National Gallery where we had spent so many happy hours together. The image on the fabric was the famous Japanese bridge scene at Giverny, which has probably been overexposed—for good reason.

"What a darling, portable souvenir," I cheered. "Just wrap it around your neck."

And I did.

The second was a beautiful book about the pre-Raphaelite painter John Millais, my favourite. On the cover was that haunting picture of Ophelia floating among the flowers. This has also been hyped over the years with posters hanging on too many walls. However, I couldn't help admiring and identifying with it—perhaps because I seemed to skim dreamily across the surface of life.

"Simone," I sputtered," this is too generous—and unnecessary. I've benefited so much from your company over the past few months. I can't believe we won't be meeting every week as usual."

"I had to show you how thankful I am," Simone responded with equal difficulty. "You've certainly livened up my life!"

"And you've done the same for me," I said, pulling a small gift—a book on architecture—from my purse.

"Oh, lovely," Simone laughed. "Now I won't be able to look at a building in this city without thinking of our exhilarating outings."

"That's quite a legacy," I replied.

I also wanted to tell Simone that her kindness and appreciation provided a nice balance to those Felt-Really-Bad Occasions I had just listed on the train but kept mum. The RTH was my other world—and I wasn't ready to reveal it to anyone quite yet. I was afraid that my secret life in Wimbledon might burst like a delicate bubble, if it was exposed to the elements of the external world.

Even the gentle ones generated by Simone.

After our meal, we continued along the High Street until we saw the pretty stretch of park called Kensington Gardens right beside Hyde Park. We then followed the wide pathway through the tall gates and toward the palace. Of course, we had to stop and admire the statue of King William III—the first royal resident back in 1689—which stood front and centre.

The Protestant William, a.k.a. Prince of Orange—the Dutch dynasty, not the fruit as I used to think in school—beat the Catholic King James II on the battlefield. Then he and his wife Mary—poor James's own daughter and William's first cousin in what was obviously a very dysfunctional family—claimed the throne and settled in England.

The palace had seen many changes since the days of William and Mary. The famous architect Sir Christopher Wren—who must have been a workaholic, building the latest version of St. Paul's Cathedral and lots of smaller churches around London—had added new wings and designed an entrance, so that guests approached under a fancy archway and clock tower.

It wasn't quite that regal for Simone and me. We entered by what seemed like a modest back door, had our bags scanned, paid our money, and were soon carrying audio guides around as we moved from room to room on the ground floor.

This part of the palace was where various royals had once had their private apartments—as opposed to their state or public apartments upstairs. Now those private apartments were the direct opposite—full of displays and crawling with sightseers like us.

We wandered, passing clothing from various eras, including hats, shoes, belts, and all the undergarment paraphernalia worn in more complicated times. There was even a Mantua dress, popular in the court of George I in the mid-1700s and familiar from films depicting the period, which gave women an extremely broad-hipped look that no one would want today. We would be forced to turn sideways to go through doorways making for a very awkward entrance.

And sitting down? Don't think so!

At the same time, Mantua dresses were supported by whalebone hoops, stiffened by heavy silver thread, and trimmed in sparkling silver lace. They must have weighed a ton.

"I'm glad we live in a time when things are more comfortable and practical," I observed.

"But not as impressive," Simone said. "I've always felt rather plain in my modern clothes."

"Not at all plain," I protested, "but certainly lighter."

There was also a display of lace making, showing the many delicate needles required to make minute intricate patterns on yards and yards of material. How time-consuming and tiring that must have been. Quite rightly, there was a moving history of the poor seamstresses who toiled for hours on end in poor light, ruining their eyesight to decorate the gorgeous gowns of royal and wealthy women.

"This is the real story behind all the glitter and elegance of our past," Simone stated. "Sometimes, I'm ever so ashamed of my predecessors. Perhaps simpler does have its advantages."

"In too many places, working conditions aren't much better now," I commented, receiving a slow, thoughtful nod. "Only they're making running shoes and children's toys."

In contrast to the historic extravagance, there was Princess Diana's relatively unadorned but striking wardrobe—or part of it. Eighteen dresses she had worn to this event or that: a little black number by Versace, a heavenly blue silk creation, highlighted when she danced with John Travolta at the White House in 1985 (on a Saturday night?), and a pink and blue silk taffeta dress from the evening when she and Prince Charles led the way on the dance floor in Melbourne, Australia, in 1988.

"Charles probably stepped on her toes," Simone sighed, "but I do like the man. He cares about our past and our future more than some."

We stood in front of Princess Di's clothing, thinking about the glamorous myths surrounding a woman the world later came to know so much better—including the sad details of her failed marriage. All those gowns, those potential Felt-Really-Good Occasions, and yet she was never truly a fairy-tale princess.

Now her dresses served as a reminder of a tragic, much-too-short life.

I began to wonder whether she could ever have "turned things around," if she had not died so young—if she had found her own RTH. She appeared to have been trying, in the face of many obstacles.

Feeling a little panicky at the memory of Diana's final, confused days, I couldn't help asking myself—again—if it was possible to undergo major transformation after a certain age. I could only hope the answer was Yes.

Although the downstairs exhibits were interesting, Simone and I were keen to see the historic royal state apartments on the second floor. To get there, we had to climb the ornate staircase built for George I, who was crowned king in 1714 after the deaths of William and Mary and the short reign of James II's other Protestant daughter Anne.

(My main knowledge of Anne's reign was that she had a charming greenhouse or orangery built behind the palace which now served tasty tea and cakes. Call me shallow.)

George I was Anne's second cousin, so technically not a front-runner for the crown, but he got the job because he was Protestant.

"Politics and religion. They are enough to make one's head spin," said Simone. "So much anger and division."

I tried to think of people I had read about or knew who had managed to balance the two. Gandhi, Martin Luther King . . . hmmmm . . . Chris? He had talked about Mental and Spiritual Development along with promoting outer peace and inner harmony. From what I'd encountered so far, he seemed to qualify.

How blessed I was—in a secular way—to be sharing his home and company!

As art lovers, we aimed for the King's Gallery, refurbished by George I. It was a lengthy hall with windows along one side and paintings along the other. On rainy days, the king took his strolls in this room with its graceful view of the gardens and parkland.

There, we especially liked the imposing copy of the famous van Dyck portrait of Charles I, one of George's many predecessors, on horseback. Gazing at Charles's neatly bearded face, I shivered at the thought of his fate as the only monarch to be executed in British history. In 1649, he was forced to step out of the second-floor window of Banqueting House, still located near the Thames on Whitehall, onto a scaffold—where he was gruesomely beheaded.

"This is giving me an overwhelming sense that we have to live life wisely, to the hilt, seize the moment, and all those upbeat phrases," I muttered more to myself than Simone. I was sure she had no idea what lay behind my words but was too tactful to pry. She would wait for me to bare all, if and when I wanted to.

Did I want to? Would I be able to? After all, how could I possibly describe what I hoped to accomplish at the RTH through those exercises and chats when I couldn't put it into words for myself?

Simone was on the lookout for the bedroom where Princess Victoria, age eighteen, had slept the night she became queen. On June 20, 1837, she was awakened at six in the morning and told that her uncle, William IV (who had no legitimate children but lots of others), had died not entirely unexpectedly.

She was now Queen Victoria.

All that responsibility for someone so young, I brooded. If it had been me with my track record, I would have dodged the position somehow—or quit after a few years. Sorry, gotta run! I've got more aimless wandering to do. Find another queen.

In any case, as Simone and I stood a few feet from the historic bed, it was difficult not to get caught up in the drama of that "really-felt-good-or-bad" instant for Victoria—especially when one of the security guards started to fill in some of the sordid details leading up to it.

The guard explained that Victoria's mother, the Duchess of Kent, had been so afraid that one of the other potential heirs to the throne would try to kill her daughter that she refused to allow her to sleep alone. (Imagine having your mother sleep in your room because a greedy relative might slit your throat!) Someone also held young Vicky's hand whenever she used the stairs—just in case she was given a perilous push.

"The poor child," said my dear friend. "It's all so excessive!"

After spending the entire afternoon roaming through history, Simone and I emerged into the modern world. The sun was setting as we walked back toward the tube station. Although we stopped in a small café for a cup of tea to extend our visit, we finally accepted the fact that Simone had to catch her train home—and we had to bid each other farewell until who knew when. (Unusually, she wasn't available the following week because of a planned holiday.)

Goodness, saying goodbye is tough, especially when you have no idea what lies ahead. We kept waving at each other as we walked in different directions. Waving and waving. She was so small and fragile. Would I ever see her again? Would I ever have another cultural buddy?

As I walked up to the RTH almost an hour later, Monet scarf flapping in the breeze, I was happy to see the living room light on and know that Chris was there, probably reading. I also noticed that the outside door was open an inch or so—always a welcoming sign—and Mozart was playing softly in the background.

Had my life coach been lonely before I moved in? I wondered. He seemed so grateful for my company.

"I'm home from the palace," I announced cheerily as I entered the cosy room, "and I have my list of Felt-Really-Bad Occasions ready for your perusal."

Chris reached up, gave my scarf an admiring tug, and took the list. "Would you like your hot drink first?" he asked.

I was glad he hadn't offered me a whisky, which might have indicated that the next workload required some fortification. I accepted, realizing that I had hardly noticed my cold all day, took off my coat, and sat in the hard-backed chair beside the recliner.

"No, no, no!" Chris shouted, as he entered the kitchen. "That's the coach's chair. You get settled in the usual place. After all, I know you've had a physically demanding day prowling around Kensington. How did it go, by the way?"

In vain, I tried to argue that I felt too greedy and spoiled taking the most comfortable seat but was soon spreading myself happily in the softness of the lounge chair, sipping from a large steaming mug, and giving a quick overview of my afternoon.

"As usual, dear Simone and I pushed ourselves to our sightseeing limit," I concluded. "But it was worth the effort. It helped me raise my head above my own concerns—or the opposite."

"It's fascinating to examine the lives of others, isn't it?" Chris observed thoughtfully. "They have so many lessons to teach us. If only we'd notice." Then it was back to business. "Shall we continue with what we started this morning?"

I told him I was definitely ready for more, since I was curious to know what he thought of my Five Occasions When I Felt Really Bad About My Actions, Behaviour, or Role. Who wouldn't be?

He began to study the list.

In spite of my enthusiasm—and the suspense—I couldn't help putting my head back, closing my eyes, and thinking again about the day's kings, queens, princes, and princesses. Those trying, sometimes-tragic lives. It was amazing how people got so wrapped up in their struggle to survive that they lost their objectivity, their bearing.

"Your Felt-Bad Occasions aren't that bad, Kathleen," Chris said finally. "There's certainly nothing here to lie awake at night regretting terribly. You are basically quite a decent person, aren't you?"

I stared at him. Did he actually want an answer?

"I . . . I . . . well, I guess. Thank you."

"I'm saying this to you because of what you wrote about your father and failing to keep him alive. I'm not a psychiatrist, but I have a feeling you've been pretty hard on yourself for that reason—and maybe others. You've kept tripping yourself up over the years, preventing yourself from getting where you should have got."

I wanted to cry. He was spot on. I had sabotaged myself almost systematically since I was old enough to do so. I'd turned down opportunities to go to good schools when my grandparents had offered, left good jobs, good homes, good men.

It was a long, broken path, strewn with the shards of my delicate ego.

"So," Chris said, almost cheerily, "let's go through these far-from-horrific Occasions, see why you felt the way you did, and figure out how you can avoid doing such things in the future. There's no sense wasting these fertile negative experiences, after all."

It was as if he had lifted a heavy load off my shoulders and soul. I had tried to be a decent person, but had made some—no, many—errors along the way. Nothing earth-shatteringly bad; not positive, productive, or what they call self-affirming either.

Now the challenge was to examine and learn from them.

"Well," I began tentatively, "I Felt Really Bad about pushing my younger sister in the water, although I didn't mean to, because I did resent her even when we were only eight and five years old. She came along and stole the show. She was so demanding of attention, and I was suddenly forced into the background. I know that consciously I didn't mean to push her but deep down I probably wanted to."

"So what can you learn from this? How can you avoid such feelings of resentment in the future?"

"Well," I said, gripping my warm mug between both hands. "I know my sister wasn't really my enemy. In fact, sometimes she's been a good friend. And she not only had me but my younger brother to contend with when she was born. She lost her father when she was two. I was five, as I've said. I suppose I should look at things from the other person's angle, appreciate their position, and act accordingly."

"Bravo!" said Chris.

We then went over the other four Occasions. It was clear that with my daughter's father and my former employer, I had simply not paid attention to their feelings or needs and should have done so. In both cases, I had acted thoughtlessly and in haste without examining my various options or theirs. I had emphasized the negative rather than the positive in the people and the situations.

As for my relationship with Julian, Chris suspected that it was a reflection of my own attitude about myself. I would never have accepted an arrangement so tenuous if I had been feeling positive and productive. People feeling "up" can generally recognize something that will bring them "down"—and they stay clear.

Finally, on my feeling bad because I hadn't been clever or resourceful enough over the past few months in London, Chris stated that, from his vantage point, I'd had an incredible time—and accomplished a fair amount.

"Considering you arrived knowing almost no one, I think you were amazingly successful. You parlayed nothing into quite a lot of something by being outgoing and friendly and, dare I say it, clever and resourceful."

"But I've ended up with so little," I insisted. "I didn't get a job or a visa; I didn't get the man I wanted; I'm almost penniless."

"Look at what you *did* do, not at what you *didn't* do. You did a lot and you can always come back and do more. There's no sense thinking the way you're thinking. It's inaccurate and gets you nowhere."

With that, Chris and I fell into a deep silence which was rare for us. He was right again. I had to start thinking constructively, rather than destructively which had always been my habit. I had to turn this negative ship of mine around and go full speed ahead in a more positive direction.

But it seemed about as manoeuvrable as the *Titanic* heading toward an iceberg! Too big and heavy to change course.

Then I remembered those royals whose lives I had spied on all afternoon. They too must have felt like they couldn't alter their course—even though their lives depended on it, in some cases. They had all the pressures of the royal court, governments, the public. I, on the other hand, was a free agent and should rejoice in that fact.

My only limitations were the ones I imposed on myself.

I went to bed with a renewed sense of determination and purpose. Even though I wouldn't be publicly condemned or executed if I didn't succeed, I knew I had to make the RTH work for me. I dozed off picturing myself in a Versace dress dancing with Julian. Not a bad start to the rest of my life, but was it a helpful one?

Round and round I went.

CHAPTER SEVEN

Be a Light

✥

Be a light unto yourself.

—Buddha

It was Saturday, Day 6. We were heading southeast of London toward the English Channel, or La Manche, the Sleeve," as the French call it in their imaginative way. Chris was an excellent driver, which came as a relief. I find it difficult to feel comfortable or remain silent when I sense that the person behind the wheel lacks basic driving know-how—and might kill or maim me.

Perhaps it's my overdeveloped instinct for survival, but some people just don't seem to have a talent for controlling fast-moving vehicles. They're missing the quick wit needed for the right response when the crunch comes—or, better still, to prevent the crunch. So I was enjoying being with an expert, not having to scrutinize the road ahead, as if I were watching for landmines.

There was something sad about the moment too. I guess the word would be "bittersweet" or "sweetbitter."

Until that day, almost all my travels outside London had been with Julian, who was also a good driver. I loved being cooped up in his little car with him, talking, laughing, reaching over to touch him. I could remember, especially, driving back in the rain one night from some picturesque village or town we'd been exploring. In spite of the fact that he couldn't see the road very well and had to concentrate on the job of getting us home alive, he had held my hand against his chest—his heart—for most of the trip.

(He was driving a manual-shift car, so imagine the challenge! True love?)

Yes, I missed Julian terribly but was determined not to dwell on the past. Appreciate the present, I reminded myself. Devour it. Learn from it. Besides, Julian and I were getting together when I returned to London on Monday.

Only two days to wait.

Speeding along the roadway in a car almost identical to Julian's, Chris didn't miss an opportunity to point out items of interest. We were traversing the grassy North Downs, he said, moulded from chalk and once covered with forests—hard to picture. These Downs lay between two areas officially considered to be of "outstanding" natural beauty—the Surrey Hills and the Kent Downs.

"They've discovered human and animal remains, along with bits of worked flint for tools, which show that this area has been inhabited for thousands of years."

"Everything in this country puts the present into such perspective—that word again," I responded, slightly awestruck. "Canada has a lengthy, rich history, particularly our First Nations, but, sadly, there's less sense of it. Here, I feel like such a newcomer."

"Aren't you?" Chris asked, as he expertly took a tight corner. "We're all new, growing, and ready to be shaped just the way we want and need. Keep that in mind."

"Whatever you say!"

He then announced that, if we followed our present route to its end, we would arrive at the fabled White Cliffs of Dover—where we probably wouldn't see bluebirds, since they were purportedly a fantasy of the American songwriter.

That wasn't our plan. We were heading farther south.

This was a quick and spontaneous weekend break from the city and all the last-minute gallivanting I had planned to do. It was also a working holiday—too tempting to resist after a full day of therapy the day before. I knew that once we'd settled into the little cottage, which Chris had rented over the Internet, I would be back on the psyche hot seat, mining my past, mind, and soul, preparing to map out my future.

Although I was looking forward to this abstract, cerebral adventure—the rural RTH—I was determined to enjoy the scenery and the unknown world around me, while I could.

As dusk began falling, we entered the town of Tenterden, in the county of Kent, with a wide boulevard running down the centre—one of those graceful High Streets lined with small gift and antiques (as they say there) shops. Large overhanging trees added to the peaceful look. A mediaeval church, St. Mildred's, seemed to stand guard over the town as it had for centuries.

Chris informed me that a beacon from the church tower had once warned locals that the hostile Spanish Armada was approaching. That was when the town had better access to the coast. Now, after the coastline had been revamped in the fifteenth and sixteenth centuries by both nature and man—incredible work in those low-tech times—it was no longer a port. Its watchdog role had disappeared, but so had the Armada!

When we found our little cottage on the edge of town, Chris backed the car into an impossibly small driveway and we walked down a narrow pathway to the back door. We were right on time.

The landlord, who had obviously been waiting for us, poked his head out with a big smile. He took us on a quick tour of the place, which dated from the era when most men—and women—were much shorter in stature. Chris was almost bent over double as we climbed the narrow stairs to the second floor.

It was worth it. We loved the half-timbered ceilings, slanted walls, and flowery wallpaper in the two bedrooms. The epitome of old-country charm.

We were also thrilled by the rustic fireplace in the living room and the supply of chopped wood lined against the wall beside it. The landlord then pointed out a few of the quirkier aspects of the house: how to get the taps to turn off completely, for example. Finally, he informed us that he would be just next door, if we ran into any "problems" and, ducking his head, left by the front entrance.

Once alone, Chris and I collapsed gratefully onto a pretty loveseat, the main piece of living-room furniture. We were in the middle of nowhere—for us—an exciting place to be.

"Care for a scotch, Kathleen?" he asked. "I think we both deserve one."

I gave him an exaggerated nod and he headed to the little kitchen. "I'm quite a good fire-builder," I yelled seconds later. "Why don't I start one? It would add to the ambience."

"Fire builder?" Chris yelled back. "I'm impressed. Why didn't you put that on your list of skills? You're holding back on me!"

"I'm holding back on myself. Haven't you noticed?"

Soon I was bunching up pages of newspaper, with the odd glance at interesting articles about minor local controversies, and piling small pieces of kindling in the shape of a badly leaning tepee. I lit one of the long matches I found in a box beside the fireplace and my structure was ablaze.

How comfortable! Everything appeared to be arranged so that the many strangers making their temporary nests there could adjust as easily as possible.

Chris handed me my drink, admired the blaze, and announced that he'd brought mussels for dinner, so I should curl up by the fire with my book while he prepared them.

"Shouldn't this be your day off?" I protested. "You've done all the cooking since I first showed up. It's not that I don't appreciate it, but I feel like I'm not pulling my weight."

"Pull it when you get back home," Chris insisted. "I haven't had a chance to spoil someone for too long, and I'm enjoying doing it as much as I hope you're enjoying receiving it. Besides, it's part of your

RTH therapy. I want you to know that you're someone who *deserves* to be treated this way. We all are, but rarely get a chance to realize it."

"Okay, Doctor," I replied, taking a sip of whisky. Goodness, this was heavenly. I was queen for a fortnight, even though my present castle could fit into a Kensington Palace cupboard.

"I'll try to get used to being royal. It seems like an ideal role, in spite of certain risks, so why not?" I moved a couple of large pillows neatly stacked on the floor closer to the fire and flopped down on them with a loud sigh. "Does that sound like appreciation?" I asked.

Because it certainly was.

We dined at a very small table that we had moved in front of the fire, emptying the mussel shells one by one until we had a hill of them in a bowl. The broth was as good as anything I had eaten in French restaurants and we both dipped several pieces of bread in to soak up every drop. Chris had also made a fresh, organic, mixed-greens salad with a vinaigrette to die for.

The rest of the evening was spent roasting in front of the hot fire and talking about whatever came to our lazy minds. It wasn't a serious conversation. That would come tomorrow, Chris warned tactfully. He wanted to introduce me to a new and essential concept—something that would completely change my way of looking at the world.

I was ready.

―※―

The following afternoon, we went for a walk along a beach by the English Channel. The wind was strong but not too loud, so we were able to talk with ease.

"I'd like to begin our next lesson, if you don't mind," Chris said. "This energetic environment inspires me to discuss substantial things!"

I told him I'd love to combine the pleasures of our wild surroundings with the business of learning more about life. It would be a potent mix.

"Alright, here goes." He smiled. "Have you ever heard of Richard Dawkins, the distinguished UK zoologist?"

"He's the author of that controversial book on atheism, *The God Delusion*, which I haven't managed to read," I replied.

My companion stepped over a large piece of very gnarled driftwood—the kind I would have liked to take home but knew wouldn't fit in either of my suitcases.

"Back in 1976, in his book *The Selfish Gene*, Dawkins invented the word '**Meme**' to describe a unit, if you will, which enables social behaviour—a preference, prejudice, or lifestyle—to be transmitted from individual to individual, group to group. This means that we can now identify the various factors that cause people to behave in certain ways—eat pizza, take piano lessons, or wear makeup, for example." I blinked, wondering if mine was smudged in all this wind. "In other words, Memes are the laws, pressures, traditions, even television programmes and films that mould and govern the way we live our lives."

"Really?" I interrupted, genuinely surprised by this odd revelation. "I've never even heard of the word. Did you say 'Memes'?"

"Yes, like genes, only Memes, with an *m*—or two," said Chris, suddenly coming to a standstill. I had the feeling he knew he had led us into complex territory yet again, and the journey wouldn't be easy.

"In fact, one way of understanding the concept of Memes is to relate it to genes. As you know, genes are the fundamental building blocks of all living things. They cause us to develop blue eyes instead of brown, blond hair instead of red, white skin instead of black. They determine *what* we are."

"Memes, on the other hand, determine *who* we are. They're the building blocks of our attitudes and beliefs," he explained with his big hands spread out in front of him. "They work on the unconscious mind to transfer what are called 'nurtured' or 'imitated' cultural behaviours. They govern our actions and reactions, cause us to like opera instead of rock, speak English instead of Chinese. They are behind the friends we make, the politicians we elect, and the wars we fight. Everything!"

"This is fascinating," I said, and I meant it. I loved uncovering what makes people tick—not just myself—and the Meme theory sounded as close as you could get. It was also a little overwhelming, but I was getting used to that with my new friend. "I hadn't realized that the transfer of lifestyle choices and values had been given a name. So would a Meme account for women of centuries ago wearing those impossible Mantua dresses I saw Thursday?"

"Exactly! You can't see them, but Memes have been there throughout human history. And they're powerful. They can even make people wear ridiculous clothes."

Chris picked up a small, baby-smooth stone and whipped it with full force toward the water where it disappeared into a breaking wave. He pointed to a bench and we sat down. He was deep into his presentation.

"Many people think that this is the single, most essential step in the birth of an entirely new scientific discipline. They also believe it will have a major impact on our society and the world in the twenty-first century. By the way, the study of Memes is called **Memetics**, like genetics. Handy, isn't it?"

"Very," was all I could manage. Anything that helped me wade through weighty material was welcome. You say genetics; I say Memetics.

"What this discovery means," Chris went on, "is that, for the first time, it's possible to isolate and manipulate the cultural forces—the conventions, rules, habits—that cause individuals and societies to adopt particular patterns. These patterns, by the way, account for about 99 percent of human behaviour."

"That doesn't leave much room for non-programmed living!"

"Precisely. Once we realize this, we can make Memes work for us, rather than against us. By identifying the forces—or Memes—that cause negative or unhealthy behaviour, **Memetic Engineering** can replace them with new Memes, leading to positive or healthy behaviour. Imagine."

"I'm imagining."

"So just as the Russian scientist Pavlov was able to cause dogs to salivate at the sound of a bell, citizens can convince politicians to listen; teachers can inspire students to learn, and so on. It's a scientific approach to the government of humankind."

"It sounds powerful."

I began to wonder if Chris saw me as some kind of Pavlovian experiment and the RTH as his secret laboratory. Would I soon be salivating at his will?

And not just over his cooking!

"Memetic Engineering basically involves finding answers to questions, such as: What makes one organization much more effective than another? What influences human beings to live for the moment, exploiting each other and the planet, rather than thinking long-term? What are the pressures that cause a state to go to war, rather than negotiate peace?

"It can provide specific solutions to many of our seemingly intractable problems. By identifying the social and cultural causes underlying negative behaviour and replacing them with the opposite, Memetic Engineers can change the way we manage the world."

"That's very ambitious," I interjected. "It means they can completely alter our lives, basically."

"Yes, they...we...can ensure that societies adopt beneficial behaviour as a matter of positively programmed choice, rather than negatively programmed habit—by capping the pay and bonuses of company executives, for example. There's a Meme change that's relevant."

"And long overdue!"

"In other words, once it catches on, this new scientific discipline of Memetics will open a radically different chapter in the history of human development. We'll have a much greater understanding of how our lives work and how to make them better."

"This is awesome," I observed, pushing some sand to one side with my shoe. It was good to feel the solidity and reliability of nature while in the midst of such a discussion—because Memetic

Engineering sounded a little frightening, like some kind of insidious mind control.

I couldn't help wondering again what it had to do with our work together.

"Yes, it is," said Chris. "I remember the first time I was told about it. I was amazed and couldn't believe what I was hearing. I'll be more specific to make things clearer. One group of Memes most of us are familiar with is related to driving—the rules, regulations, and procedures associated with handling a car safely.

"As we cruise along the road, we're constantly responding to the world around us by way of these Memes. If a traffic light turns red, we bring the car to a halt, and move off when the light turns green. We automatically apply the brakes, press the gas pedal, and use the indicators; we turn on the lights when it gets dark.

"Most driving behaviours have developed into habitual routines governed by unconscious, learned responses, available whenever they're needed. The actions and reactions take place without our having to think about them."

"I've had times when I can't remember anything about the past few miles I've driven because I've been daydreaming so much," I confessed.

"Exactly. It's as if the conscious mind, having made the decision to drive, switches off, and we revert to the unconscious. The same goes for every repetitive role or activity in life. Whether we are a doctor, journalist, world traveller, or parent, we all develop programmes and patterns of behaviour that enable us to carry out a wide range of activities automatically. As I said, 99 percent of the time we are in unconscious, auto-response mode."

"That's definitely a large part of our lives," I said. "It's quite disconcerting. Do we really spend that much time on automatic pilot? If so, it means that we aren't usually in complete control of . . . most things. It could be dangerous."

"You're right. These response patterns and programmes apply to every aspect of our lives—and they're not necessarily beneficial.

Memes are mindless and don't judge whether a particular response is good or bad, right or wrong, legal or illegal. They can cause us to adopt certain behaviours without any regard to their value."

"But what can we do about it?"

Chris turned to me with a smile. "As with all habits, this Meme-driven programming continues until something powerful enough convinces a person or society to look for an alternative."

"Like being thrown out of the UK?"

"You betcha. With the example of driving a car, we know how the sudden appearance of a speed camera or police car makes us check our speed and, if necessary, slow down. The 'over-fast' driving programme or Meme that had unconsciously taken control is rapidly and consciously replaced by a 'legal-speed' one."

I wanted to tell Chris that I thought his driving Memes were excellent, conscious or unconscious, but he was in full explanatory throttle now.

"As I mentioned, Memetic Engineering is the process of devising and introducing influences which cause people to react or respond in a new, predictable, and, ideally, more constructive way. Can you think of an example where it could be applied?"

"Yes, actually," I said, indicating a plastic bottle lying in the sand. "If there were deposits on food and drink containers, customers would have more incentive to return them in good condition for re-use. This would cut down on the garbage tossed everywhere, and landfill sites, as well as the energy needed to produce more packaging."

"We'd save precious resources and cut CO_2 emissions, too," Chris added. "All it would take is getting rid of the 'one-trip-packaging' Meme and replacing it with the 'reusable-packaging' one."

"Would that be the Green Meme?" I teased. "Seriously, the possibilities are endless and good—if they're used by the right people for the right reasons. What about Memes on an individual level—in terms of changing your own life?"

I could tell he was expecting this question.

"Just as we're able to switch from one television programme to another by pressing a button on the TV controller, so we can switch our own behaviour programmes—our Memes—with the press of a mental-controller button."

"Surely it can't be that easy."

"Indeed, it is, Kathleen. It has to be. The conscious replacement of an inappropriate, potentially harmful, programmed behaviour with an appropriate, beneficial one is the key to human survival and progress. We have to know how to change! The wise and skilful person develops an understanding of her own habitual behaviours and, by pressing the right 'buttons,' she can take control of her patterns and thoughts."

"This *does* sound good," I observed cautiously. "Inspiring. We can become aware of our Memes and change them to meet our real needs. There is hope yet again!"

"Yes," Chris responded. "Memetic Engineering is all about controlling our unconscious mind. It's very empowering. We can identify those heavily ingrained, negative programmes and switch them off or substitute them with new and better ones. I call it **Personal Process Analysis**. By learning to manage our Memes, we can regain control of our mental processes and steer them in a way that's beneficial, rather than harmful.

"In other words, we can park the negative Memes that cause us to emphasize everything that's wrong with our lives—the failures, the difficulties, the weaknesses in ourselves and others—and replace them with positive ones, emphasizing what's right—the accomplishments, the successes, the skills, strengths, and qualities. The result? We turn ourselves around and become much nicer, more motivated people."

That was certainly preferable, I concluded inwardly. I would have loved to take all of my negative, self-critical, failure-obsessed Memes and park them right at the top of one of those ugly, multi-level, concrete garages you find in most modern cities—for good.

"Another metaphor which I find quite useful," Chris continued, "is comparing us to a computer. The brain is a human being's hardware, whereas the programmed mind is the software. When our old software programmes are out-of-date or no longer helpful, we can substitute them. We don't necessarily have to give up on the computer itself."

"That's good to know," I said with a laugh, "because it would be pretty bizarre exchanging our brains for a new model. Imagine the line-ups at the return counter!"

Then more solemnly, "I really like this. As you say, it's very empowering when you have a clear concept of being able to change your Memes—re-programme your software."

"I thought you'd be interested, once I'd given you a sense of the power of the Meme beast. For example, you want to improve your professional life. In order to do this, we have to establish what influences have affected you negatively and deal with them. Toss them out!"

"There are so many. It's difficult to know where to begin," I moaned. My self-pitying Meme was alive and well. "Aren't we searching for several needles in several haystacks? I don't know which Memes I'd want to deal with first."

"That's one reason I've been trying to get you to know yourself better," Chris explained. "We're such complicated creatures, such mysteries to ourselves. You're right. We have to sort through a lot of haystacks, but, if you truly want to change, we have to keep plugging away as methodically and scientifically as possible. Find those hidden needles."

I shifted more sand, building a small pile between both feet. There was something reassuring about all those teeny-tiny bits of rock, crushed eons ago. Like my history lessons at Kensington Palace and driving across ancient countryside, they put my little problems—and even my Memes—into humbling context.

Once, I'd heard that there were more stars in the cosmos than there are grains of sand on the planet. How utterly mind-boggling! Infinity really is beyond comprehension. In fact, life and the universe are so complex and diverse you have to wonder how we insignificant humans can possibly make sense of them—or ourselves.

But we've got to try!

"I'm so happy to have you guiding me through the first steps of this process," I told Chris. "I've made hit-or-miss attempts in the past—or, more accurately, just miss—but this time I'm determined to make progress, and it's all because of you and the RTH. Isn't it strange how fate intervenes?"

"Fate or something." Chris stood up. "Now let's head to Dungeness and buy some fresh scallops right off the boat. We can't miss such a seaside opportunity."

Realizing the serious part of the afternoon had come to an end, I rose and shook the sand from my shoes. "That sounds divine. I don't know what Meme has made me love scallops, but it's one idiosyncrasy I *don't* want to change. In fact, all my shellfish-loving Memes are keepers. By the way, I said shellfish, not selfish!"

CHAPTER EIGHT

What I Do

I will act as if what I do makes a difference.
—William James

As we walked back toward the car, Chris bent over and picked up something off the beach.

"I've been looking for these since we first arrived and finally found one. Here's a souvenir of our time here." He handed me a rough, donut-shaped stone, like a small napkin ring. "Imagine the forces that had to work away to create such an unlikely shape. Fortunately, nature is more patient than we humans. It doesn't insist on perfection in the first instance."

I rolled the white, grey, and brown token around in my hand; I peered through the hole in its centre. Chris was right. It had taken centuries of slow natural processes to produce this little gem. How could I expect to transform myself overnight?

"Okay. I get it," I said. "I'll keep this as a reminder to be equally patient, as I try to wear away some of those negative influences."

We drove to Dungeness and found a small shack near the shoreline, lit up in the fading day. Two fishermen were working in the area to one side of the front door, beheading a large bloody freshly caught fish. They nodded as we passed, and I'm sure they couldn't miss the look of horror on my all-too-urban face.

Inside the tiny building, a round rosy woman stood behind a counter displaying the catches of the day—including plaice, which seemed popular for fish and chips. (I had seen a shop in London cleverly called My Plaice.) Chris and I pointed to the fleshiest scallops and, after some small talk about the weather, returned to the car with our "catch" and aimed for home.

First, we had to visit a few pubs. After all, the British countryside and villages are still dotted with them—although too many have closed in recent years—and you simply can't miss the variety of ambiances they offer.

We stopped at a couple of distinctive spots with uneven low ceilings and a few locals hanging around the bar, who greeted us politely as we entered. In each, we ordered a regional beer on tap, chatted awhile together or with the strangers, and continued down the road.

Our last stop was the best, the Mermaid Inn in the once-seaside town of Rye. After parking nearby, Chris and I wandered along winding streets covered in beach pebbles, instead of the usual dull asphalt, and lined with crooked buildings illuminated by strings of twinkling lights. It was like fairyland!

Finally, we arrived at the inn, painted Tudor white between the exposed black timbers. Its leaded windows glowed with a soft yellow light from inside—and seemed to welcome us and any travellers. A small sign by the entrance announced that the structure had been modernized in the 1400s.

Obviously, it was cutting edge, we joked, as Chris pulled the old door open. We followed a dark hallway to the inn lounge with its huge blazing fireplace and sat down at a table almost dangerously close to the flames. There weren't too many people around, but there was lots of character. I felt I had been dropped into an untouched scene from the past.

As is the way in many British pubs, Chris wandered up to the bar to order something—on tap. Table service often seemed optional and I was always amazed at how patient Britons were, as they stood waiting to be looked after.

I took advantage of my time alone to examine the inglenook, adjoining the fireplace, bordered on either side by adorable benches. Over the past centuries, I imagined, many rustic types must have sat themselves down there to dry off after a wet day of farming, hunting, or simply hiking through the fields.

If only the cramped little nooks could talk! They might help me evaluate my present and future in a more practical, down-to-earth, mud-on-your-boots way.

No nonsense.

More likely, they'd consider me a rather silly, spoiled creature, the product of far-easier times—which wouldn't do much good for my peace of mind!

Chris and I stayed in this perfect place for a long while, unable to leave. It was one of those discoveries that you don't want to part from, knowing you will miss it almost instantly.

"I misspent my youth not far from here," Chris confessed during our comfortable conversation, "tearing aimlessly along country roads with my pals. It was wild, futile, even dangerous. I wanted you to know the area—and more about me."

His first real job was buying and selling antiques, and he got to know every highway and byway while searching for treasures from the past. It had been a fun, lucrative way to make a living in those pre-eBay days. He'd even had his own shop just down the road from where we were.

Then an older man—obviously seeing qualities Chris himself had not yet appreciated—had offered him a job with a large firm, teaching team-building and doling out strategic personnel advice to corporations. It was there that he began his search for answers to the troubling questions his younger self had been trying to ignore.

"Even after I finally left the job," he told me, "I knew I'd never be able to look at life and human actions and interactions in the same way. So, through reading, counselling, and co-counselling, I've continued to educate myself in this area. I find it satisfying because, as I try to help others, I learn things that I hope will help me as well."

He smiled. "So you see, my guiding you through your difficult time is selfish—nothing more. I hope you don't feel exploited, Kathleen."

Although I realized he was joking, I let him know that I could handle a lot more of this kind of exploitation. Who couldn't?

"Use me as much as you want," I almost cried, but thought better of it.

Finally, we left the Mermaid Inn and drove home—to our cottage, our own little piece of history. Once again, I was on fire-building duty, after making such a good impression the evening before with my Girl Guide know-how.

What other accomplishments or skills had I forgotten about or underrated? I wondered, as I packed balls of newspaper together. I liked the idea that I could be underestimating myself terribly—and there were all sorts of goodies ready to surface as my self-awareness expanded. On the other hand, I might have hit rock bottom with my exploratory shovel.

Perhaps all the jewels had already been mined.

No, I told myself, shaking my head as I lit the fire, I wasn't going to think that way. I wasn't going to allow my high spirits to be pulled down by my habitual negativity. Go away, self-doubting memes! Scram!

Chris, in the kitchen oblivious to my internal battle, cooked up the scallops and poured us some chilled white wine. When we sat down to eat at the small table, moved in front of the fireplace, they were so tender and juicy I almost moaned in appreciation—and, afterward, wanted to scour the cottage for a cigarette.

Yes, it has been another stimulating, informative, and sensuous day, I thought contentedly as we relaxed, watching the fire leap about. I knew I could get to like this combination.

"Before declaring today over," Chris said after a long, slow sip of wine, "I'm wondering if you'd like to do another exercise. You seem in a mellow-enough mood to be particularly honest with yourself, so I think this would be a good time for it."

I smiled submissively, too happy and satisfied to object to anything. He could have asked if I minded having my wisdom teeth extracted by firelight! Just prop your head on this pillow and open your mouth wide. I'll get the pliers. Now say, "Ah."

Ahhhhh . . .

My life coach rose from the table and dug a printed piece of paper and a pen out of his briefcase. He always seemed ready and eager, this man, to put me through my mental and spiritual paces.

The paper was headlined **Characteristics of an Ideal Human Being**. Underneath, there were two columns, each with about fifty Characteristics—from Compassionate to Imaginative to Brave. I was required to rate myself on a scale of one—for a low grade—to five.

Chris picked up our plates, clearing a workspace on the table. Without a word, he left me to my thoughts and self-assessment and almost tiptoed to the kitchen to perform his domestic chores.

As in other exercises, I tried not to over-think, double-think, or second-guess and, with the help of my wine intake, I began jotting down numbers beside the wide variety of Characteristics. "Compassionate, 4. Loving, 4. Enthusiastic, 4." Was I being too modest, or, God forbid, too generous?

No doubting allowed!

I moved rapidly down one row and jumped across to the next, ending with "Articulate, 4. Accepting, 3.5." Typically, just as I came to an almost-breathless halt at the bottom of the page, Chris was by my side.

"Well done," he said, picking up my latest confessional. "First of all, I'm impressed by the speed with which you filled this out. You apparently have quite a sense of or feel for yourself and are able to self-assess fairly quickly. That's a good start. Most people can't.

"Second, I don't see any really low grades, which is also positive. No irrational self-hate. That's always valuable. It's good to be your own friend, rather than foe. Now let's look at the patterns."

"Ah, those revealing patterns," I teased. "Where would we be without them?"

We started with my lowest estimations of myself. I had given Purposeful, Ambitious, Motivated a 2.5. Then for some reason, I gave Realistic, Recognizes Talents, Learns from Success (not so far), and Dedicated a 2.8—a compromise grade.

Climbing up the scale to 3, there were traits like Motivational (I seemed to be able to help others more than myself), Leader (ditto), Rational (sometimes). I granted myself 3.5 to Trusting, Respectful, Generous, Thoughtful, Sensitive, Observant, Reliable, Selfless, Encouraging, Constructive, Helpful, Faithful (when warranted), Charitable (ditto), and Self-Worth (not too low a grade, given the context).

"See any of those patterns yet?" I interrupted, barely avoiding the temptation to tug at Chris's shirt sleeve. "I think I do."

"That's good. That's very good. But let's keep going. I think the best is yet to come."

I gave a 4 grade to some pretty important qualities: Trustworthy, Honest, Truthful, Creative, Supportive, Shows Feelings (Boy, do I! So why didn't I give it a 5?), Caring, Considerate, Co-operative, Intelligent, Kind, Energetic, Imaginative, Charming (or so I've been told), Witty (I do make people laugh), Loyal (sometimes much too), Joyous (I still loved life in spite of the fact that it totally confused me!).

The highest mark I was willing to give myself was 4.5. Never perfect in my own estimation. I wondered what Chris thought of that. In this privileged category, I placed Courageous (after the past six months, of course), Willing to Learn (ditto), Value-Driven, Stands Up for Values, Challenges.

"My goodness," Chris murmured, shaking his head like a doctor examining the x-ray of a long-time smoker. "So, what patterns have you seen?" he asked, throwing the diagnosis over to me.

I took a deep breath and went for it. "Well, I seem to have a very low sense of my ability to act—be purposeful or ambitious—even though I have a lot of courage and drive. Ouch."

"Yes, Kathleen, you do span the spectrum!" Chris said. "And in between, you've acknowledged in yourself all the necessary Characteristics required to be a decent human being. No underestimation there! I guess the next step is to find out how we can bring that lack of purpose and ambition up a few notches to match your character. Shall we begin tomorrow?"

With that, we watched as the fire slowly faded and I quietly stewed about the following day, which I knew would be challenging. I would be seeing Julian—my nemesis—for the first time in more than a week. Would the past few days with Chris make my time with my Highgate amour any different than it had been since we met?

That question was something to sleep—or, more accurately, toss and turn—on. I feared the answer was No.

CHAPTER NINE

Your Very Best

*As long as you are trying your very best,
there can be no question of failure.*
—Mahatma Gandhi

I am not an early-morning person by habit, choice, or meme-programming, but Chris and I were up and at 'em at a very respectable hour the next day. This required a good strong cup of coffee in order to focus eyes and thoughts.

Because I rarely come in contact with large doses of caffeine, the odd times when I *do* allow it to enter my body—especially on an empty, unsuspecting stomach—have a powerful effect. My nervous system speeds up, and I become a trembling fireball of energy—super-awake, alive, high.

Typically—perhaps naively, under the circumstances—Chris had a post-coffee, post-breakfast, pre-heading-home task for me (or us). He suggested that, in light of my impending reunion with Julian, I do a couple of awareness exercises to fortify myself with something more substantial than a potent brown liquid.

Right! Great idea! I was keen. More self-awareness was never out of place. I grabbed a pen—my newfound weapon against self-delusion and ignorance. Where was some paper? I was ready to go.

"Steady. Easy does it," laughed Chris, his hands raised in front of him, forming a protective barrier. "I like enthusiasm, but this is too much!"

"I might be in overdrive, zoom, zoom. But I can think straight," I promised. "And I'm genuinely eager to get started."

Chris placed a blank sheet of paper in front of me. "Last night, you graded yourself on the various Characteristics of an Ideal Human Being," he began. "Now I'd like you to write down your **Top Ten Values or Standards**—the criteria by which you measure yourself.

"Remember when we discussed the four areas of development, which included mental and spiritual? Well, until last night, most of what we've done has been in the former category. This exercise comes under the latter."

"Does this mean I've passed my mental development courses with flying colours?" I joked, and then indicated that I didn't expect—or want—a response.

Values? Standards? Not for the first time, I felt I'd been hit between the eyes by oddly foreign concepts. Of course, I had such things. Didn't I? I guided my life by them, I assumed. But when it came to writing a list, what on earth were they?

As Chris pointed out, the previous night's exercise had helped me acknowledge several abstract characteristics, such as compassionate and respectful, and had identified some of my stronger and weaker ones. But my Values and Standards—those simple little lights along the dark path or journey of existence—what were they? I knew I should be more familiar with them than I was. In fact, I should always be aware of them, as I went through life, to help me make the right decisions.

"I'll leave you alone for a while," Chris said, as he headed outside with our suitcases to the car. "Dig down. They exist. You make use of them constantly."

I sat on the loveseat by the fireplace, now filled with the ashes of the two nights of our stay. My mind seemed similarly grey and wasted. Burnt out. No, I couldn't think that way. It was destructive. Arrest that negative meme!

Agitated, I started to write, "Being open to communication." "Accepting constructive criticism." "Showing love for others."

Were these my Values or just what I valued? Or were they the same? I couldn't believe I had never thought about this before.

"Being politically principled." "Intellectual honesty."

Was I being intellectually honest at this point? I confronted myself silently. Goodness, it was so darned easy to confuse and confound oneself.

"Wisdom." "Thoughtfulness." "Generosity." "Adventurousness." Was there such a word? "Respecting nature." "Respecting others." "Respecting myself." They were related but tumbled out in that order. "Courage." That often emerged in my list-making reveries. "Decency." "Integrity."

I heard low laughter beside me. "You've done it again," said Chris. "You hesitate at the starting gate, and then race down the track to a glorious finish. In fact, you keep running—even after you cross the finish line! That's more than Ten Values and Standards. How does it feel now that you've pulled them out of yourself?"

"As usual, I love it," I declared happily, almost flinging the pen across the room. "I adore tunnelling down into the depths of my mind and soul, and coming up with all these treasures I didn't know existed. I can't believe I haven't identified my Values before! How could I live so unconsciously?"

"Most of us do," Chris responded. "We simply don't have or don't give ourselves the time to look, really delve."

"I like the word 'delve.' It sounds gentle but effective—like you!"

Chris took the page from my hand. "You are consistent, even though you've never noticed or made use of it. People, politics, intellect, courage, adventure, respect, integrity.

"Now I know we have to leave soon for your date, but would you mind writing down your **Five Main Positive Characteristics from**

Others' Point of View? Some of these will coincide with your own perceptions of yourself, but another 'perspective' is helpful. What do you think others value about you? Julian included."

What, indeed! For the past half year, I had been bouncing my personality off those of so many other human beings. What had they liked when they came in close contact with me, a total stranger? I wrote down "Sociable." Someone had once told me I was easy to connect with. Too easy? Stop! "Dynamic." I loved to be active, go places, absorb information, dance, even sing—though my voice wasn't worth listening to. "Free Spirit." Again, that sense of adventure. "Good Conversationalist."

And finally, "Quite Kind." I wasn't anything close to Mother Teresa, but I did try to be empathetic and considerate.

I returned the paper to Chris.

"You seem so ready to do and be something," he said, after reading it. "We're going to have to get working on some practical techniques to make that happen once you are back in Canada."

I cringed at the thought of "back in Canada." I knew it would be a greater challenge than what I had been going through over the past six months—in part, because it was being forced on me.

"For now," he added, "please just try to have a sense of yourself and your Values—and value the whole package. You shouldn't sell yourself short. Nobody should."

Two hours later, I was walking toward the dark little pub at the end of a hidden laneway where Julian and I often met before we went out for lunch. On the way back to London, I had tried, probably too earnestly, to prepare myself to be with the man who had dominated so much of my recent life. I had even written down some interesting thoughts and events that had cropped up since the last time we saw each other—in order to have some sense of control over what came out of my mouth.

More positively, I simply loved to share my news with Julian; he was such an appreciative listener and audience.

Pulling open the heavy pub door, I wondered if he would already be part of the regular noon-hour crowd gathered to share a pint and chat. We usually met in the back room just across from the fireplace, so I made my way there looking above the other heads as I went.

Ah, yes. There he was. I could see his slightly curly, sandy hair, the trusty trench coat over his broad shoulders. My heart started to pound just a little. I would stay calm, I promised myself.

Julian smiled his wide, generous smile the instant our eyes met and I knew he was as happy to see me as I was to see him. In spite of this, I still couldn't quell my feeling of uncertainty—and relax. Playing it cool and casual was the opposite of what I felt, so my actions weren't at all easy or natural.

"Strained" would describe them.

In reality, I wanted to fling my arms around his neck and declare my abiding love, but that was a definite no-no. He was like a skittish deer that had roamed out of the woods for a nibble of grass and didn't know whether to trust the friendly two-legged creature it kept encountering—or run for cover.

(I knew too well that Julian's first instinct over the past few months was to turn and run.)

He gave me a big hug and, like Chris, asked what I wanted to drink so he could wander up to the bar and order us something. I appreciated this ritual at that point. It gave me time to gather my thoughts.

When Julian returned, I asked about the classical guitar lesson he had had before our meeting and he pulled out some sheet music for the Bach piece he was learning. Soon, I was lost in our smooth, unconscious conversation with no sense of what my purpose or goal was with this man—and no desire whatsoever to adjust the status quo.

That was the way the afternoon went. While interacting with someone—especially that someone—away from Chris, I wasn't at all good at remembering his meme-changing advice about switching negatives to positives or even valuing myself. Evidently, it would take more RTH time and practice for me to become fully conscious of what was going on—and not simply slip into familiar and comfortable ways, even when they weren't working.

For lunch, Julian took me to Rules, established in 1798 and considered the oldest restaurant in the Covent Garden area—in all London. We found ourselves in a well-preserved memento of England past—with low lighting, large fireplaces, oil paintings and antlers on the walls, and a glass dome above. Even as a quasi-vegetarian, I loved this place, which specialized in wild game, oysters, and traditional puddings.

We were led to a private corner table—my favourite seating arrangement—and slid ourselves onto the plush banquette. There, we would stay nestled, drinking Campari and soda—not very British, but we were multicultural—before we shared a good bottle of wine and some hearty food.

After we ordered, Julian asked me about life in Wimbledon and I tried to describe the exercises I was going through with Chris. When he raised his eyebrows skeptically, I raised my glass in a mock gesture of good cheer. I wasn't going to be cowed or have my appreciation of the RTH undermined. My grasp of its concepts was weak enough!

As the booze started to stir up my thoughts again, I decided to raise a contentious issue between Julian and me after lunch. The fact was that, just before Wimbledon, I had tried to end our confusing relationship—thinking it would be better to leave the country with a clean emotional slate.

Toss the doubts and uncertainties of the past months out for good!

When I had told Julian it was over, he tried calling several times, but I refused to answer the phone. A real display—albeit temporary—of backbone. For a few miserable days, I had sincerely wanted to be free of this romantic roller coaster ride leading nowhere. Julian wanted me, but not as a real part of his life.

Finally, he sent an email with the subject heading "Message from Purgatory," saying he would be at our usual pub after his guitar lesson and "if a person I love comes along, I will take her out for lunch."

I came along. So there I was, proving just how much resolve I didn't have. It was all too obvious that my ability to avoid seeing Julian was about as likely as a blade of grass not bending in the wind.

When I mentioned our little contretemps, as we lolled about after our delicious meal, Julian simply said that he didn't want to discuss our relationship. "We've been over everything many times," he told me softly but insistently. "Nothing has changed for me. I like being on my own. We are different that way."

"You're right about that," I admitted. "When I love, I want to be with that person as much as possible, especially when it is clear how much we enjoy each other's company." I hesitated only slightly before adding, "You've said you love me."

"Let's change the subject, shall we?" he said, tears welling in his eyes. "This has never got us anywhere in the past. We should just enjoy our time together. We don't have much of it left."

Why do you want to condemn us both to "purgatory"? I wanted to yell in the centre of this hallowed British eatery. Why not allow us to love and be happy?

But I said nothing. I too didn't want to waste any more of our precious time. Julian was right, I supposed. We had discussed "us" over and over again—and I had proven myself incapable of moving the debate beyond the barriers that had stood in our way for months. Whatever programmes or memes that had convinced Julian to stay single and avoid the twists and turns of real emotional commitment were more powerful than I was.

Of course, the fact that he had told me bluntly one day that my "unstable" lifestyle made him nervous had to be factored in as well! He didn't want someone who might become "dependent." I had argued that I would work if I had the right immigration papers, and so on. But let's face it: The whole mess was one more reason to have myself thoroughly RTHed.

Foolishly, I spoke my mind and heart afresh—very fresh—a few hours and drinks later. "Why don't we go back to your place," I suggested after we had whiled away the rest of the afternoon in a nearby wine bar. "As you said earlier, we don't have much time left, so let's make the most of it."

It had been a delightful, aimless reunion—and I had, true to form, eventually thrown my arms around him. He hadn't pulled back, but was now claiming that he had to return to Highgate.

Alone.

"It would just make things more difficult when you leave next Monday," he said. "It's going to be hard enough as it is."

How different we were! I wanted to carpe diem, seize the day, the night—no matter how much pain it would cause—and he wanted to protect himself. Was there a right or wrong here? Who knew?

So, we walked hand in hand to Leicester Square Tube Station, stood on the sidewalk, jostled by passersby, and began the usually long process of saying goodbye.

"Please go," he pleaded suddenly.

I eyed him questioningly for about three seconds, and then turned and ran down the steps into the bowels of the underground without looking back. I didn't stop until I reached the turnstiles. My heart was filled with sorrow, but there was definitely a tinge or more of anger. Why did he keep rejecting me, pushing me away? And why did I keep asking for more?

The rut I was in seemed deeper and darker than ever.

❧

Thank goodness the tube ride to Wimbledon was a long one. It gave me time to semi-recuperate.

When I finally made my way back to the RTH, Chris had once more left the front door slightly ajar, anticipating my arrival. He was sitting in his reading chair, having, as usual, left the recliner available for me. I tried to cover up the sense of emptiness that had plagued me after leaving my erstwhile lover—knowing I wouldn't see him until the day I flew home.

(Oddly enough, in spite of our showdown before we parted, Julian had insisted on driving me to the airport. That was certainly something to look forward to, but how could I make it through the next lonely week?)

After a short chat about nothing very much, Chris grabbed the bull that was charging around the small living room by the horns.

"You don't seem very happy," he said. "Would you mind if I give you a little advice on how to handle days like today—those times when you want to be prepared for certain situations and learn from them afterward? I don't mean that you should be manipulative or calculating, but it might help to be more aware of what you really feel and want. It's better than simply drifting through events without some sense of your own real emotions and needs."

"Oh please, yes," I said mournfully. "I'm tired of not knowing what I want from Julian and so many other things. I'm fed up with just winging life. I don't want to be scheming or unspontaneous, but isn't there a happy medium between that and being a complete, incompetent, emotional klutz?"

"Remember how we talked about memes yesterday?" Chris asked. "Well, it's not inauthentic to examine your programming and change it for the better. We can look at this in more depth later, but, for tonight, I'd like to share a couple of easy exercises that could help. I wanted to tell you before you saw Julian, but I thought it would be too much to absorb under the circumstances."

"No doubt," I muttered.

He told me about the concept of **Sub-Personality Management**, which entailed paying close attention to what we consider habits or even vital parts of our personality. These, he said, could be adjusted or totally overruled with conscious effort.

Since I was quite down, post-Julian, he suggested I begin with what he called "**3, 2, 1 Reviewing**." After an afternoon like the one I'd just spent, I should think of Three Things That Went

Right—positive—and Two Things That Went Wrong—negative. Finally, I should come up with One Thing I Would Change for the next time—hopeful, focussed.

"Just one?" I asked.

A second method for dealing with the Julians of my life was what he called: **PARI—Plan, Act, Review, Improve**.

Before an event, such as a get-together with someone who caused a certain amount of emotional or psychological confusion, I should actively Plan what I hoped to get out of it. Armed this way, I should try to Act accordingly, as I threw myself into the proverbial lion's den. Afterward, I should Review what had transpired as honestly as possible, and try coming up with a few actions which would lead me to Improve in any future encounter.

"Plan, Act, Review, Improve," I repeated in a mantra-like drone. My booze-ridden afternoon was probably all too obvious to Chris, but he was handling it in his naturally patient way.

"I adore both these suggestions," I noted. "They sound like they would give me a fighting chance to get off the merry-go-round I've been on with Julian—fun though it is, moving up and down on those painted horses with him!"

Why did fairground analogies always seem appropriate? Was it because many of them involved going around dizzily in circles over familiar territory—the same old same old?

That was me.

Before I went upstairs, Chris had one more item on his agenda. How would I like to go to Scotland the following weekend? His son—from his first family—was getting married in a castle on the east coast and, rather than going alone as he had planned, he'd be honoured to have me join him. His treat. We could take the train up on Friday and come back Sunday—carrying on with our exercises whenever possible.

"I'd love to!" I shouted with thankfulness and relief.

Although I didn't say anything to Chris, I knew this would be the ideal way to escape from the ghost of Julian, who was always so near in London and yet so far. It meant rushing to see friends even more than I had planned, and I would have to do some major rescheduling, but I couldn't believe my luck.

I needed to flee. My heart wanted distance at the same time that it feared being apart. And voila—intriguing Scotland! Yes, sometimes the energy forces swirling around and through us had a way of dealing the perfect hand just when the poker game was becoming particularly challenging and bleak.

CHAPTER TEN

Multitudes

I am large; I contain multitudes.
—Walt Whitman, *Leaves of Grass*

With visions of Scotland hanging in the air at the RTH like a thick mist from the sea, Chris and I got down to work the next morning. Before getting on the train Friday, we had three days to wrap up several exercises, which Chris had outlined on a large piece of paper attached to an easel he had pulled out from somewhere. Using block letters, highlighting, underlining, stars, bullets, and the like, he sketched out what he wanted us to accomplish before we proceeded to King's Cross Station and parts north.

From my lounge perch, feet almost higher than my head, I, in turn, summarized my ideal social schedule before I boarded the plane in less than a week—hoping I didn't sound like too much of a butterfly in this regard. Somehow, we managed to put together a schedule that satisfied both my enthusiasm to change my life for the future and my strong desire to live for the moment.

Juggling, anyone?

Needless to say, it would make for a lot of dashing around London and well beyond, but we both thought the stretch geographically and psychologically was worth it.

Knowing I was heading that afternoon to visit my long-time friend Lori and her family in the village of Hampton Hill, followed by a rendezvous with my newer pal Leila, Chris wasted no time—after we had figured out how much of it was available.

"I'm wondering if you'd like to start by writing down a few words about **Who You Are**," he said. "Imagine you're on a train or plane—you'll be on both over the next while—and you're quickly describing yourself to the stranger next to you. You can be very honest because you won't ever see this person again. A brief summary is all you need, combining the good and the less good. I don't want your life story. Simply Who You Are."

"Who I am?" I asked, bewildered. Or who am I?

Had I ever really asked *that* question with any seriousness? And now that I was, how could I sum myself up in a few short sentences? Not long before the RTH, I'd been reading about the concept of being authentic and true to yourself, but who was *myself*? What did I consist of? What was the essence or gist—an odd word—of *me*?

After all, if I didn't know, how could I be even remotely authentic and true to *me*, *myself*, and *I*?

As Chris headed upstairs, I closed my eyes and let random images and impressions roam through the hills and valleys of my mind. I was slowly getting used to the art of going beyond my usual layers of thought. In part, this was because, as Chris had pointed out, I was learning to concentrate and be more aware of what was inside, deep inside, my head, heart, and even my soul.

I was becoming a better digger.

Now I aimed my newfound ability at my latest challenge. What words describe Kathleen? Who is she?

Finally, I took a deep breath and started to write. "I am a friendly, outgoing, easygoing person who loves travel, adventure, and meeting people."

Good start, but what else? I closed my eyes again and listened to my breathing. And then, "I have strong values and opinions about life and the world, but, for some reason, I can't seem to focus on anything in order to be grounded and stable. Therefore, I'm not very productive or respected for my work. Even though I regret this deeply, I can't seem to change."

I almost added, "Please, stranger-on-the-train, help me!" But I realized I had already found a stranger who lived beside the tracks and was not only devoting his precious time to helping me find myself but was about to take me on a lengthy train ride to Scotland. How many saviours did a woman really need?

Many, I told myself, if she keeps avoiding doing anything for herself.

I continued: "Although I have reasonably good relationships with those close to me, I feel I am not truly engaged with them or life. I am caring but scattered, and can't quite offer people any kind of real, solid presence. I want to be more artistic and intellectual in my life, but spend most of it dealing with survival issues. It's a kind of vicious circle. I don't focus, so I don't succeed. I don't succeed, so I don't have the wherewithal to focus. Help!"

A few minutes after dropping my pen on my lap, I heard Chris coming down the stairs. Would he be able to tell what a stew I was in? I wanted to crumple up the paper I'd been writing on, lob it across the room, and tell him to forget about the whole "Me" project. It was too much work and effort. Too invasive. Too true.

Or was this attitude of avoiding uncomfortable challenges the crux of my problem?

Chris sat down beside me. "Your summary seems to have put you in a bad state. I'm sorry. I certainly didn't want that to happen. I just wanted you to look at yourself in capsule form. We've had several exercises trying to burrow down and discover your various attributes and experiences, so I thought you might want to sum things up."

"I summed things up, alright. Too well. I have these strengths that are sabotaged by multiple weaknesses. It's as simple as that." I handed Chris what I had written. He read it and smiled his usual kind smile.

"This is good. And yes, we still have some work to do. Now I'd like you to write down **Your Ideal Life**. What would you like to have, if you could pull yourself together? And you will! Again, nothing too long."

My Ideal Life? With all the complaining I had done over the years about this person, job, or place *not* being quite right, had I ever identified what it was I wanted? In so many words?

Chris went to the kitchen, saying he was going to make us a light lunch before I left. I lay my head on the padded back of the chair and closed my eyes. The absolutely *best* life for me. What would it be?

I knew I wasn't dreaming of big houses, cars, fur coats, or chumming with wealthy people in private clubs. What I'd seen and done of that wasn't very appealing—too materialistic, empty, and purposeless—but I did like a little glamour now and then. The odd encounter with the famous, especially those who had accomplished something for humankind, added spice.

I turned over the Who I Am piece of paper and slowly but surely came up with an opening line.

"My Ideal Life would be to write books, articles, and opinion columns that are respected and valued, and help improve the world and people's lives in some way."

I stared out the window at the fence hiding the trains and their tracks. All was silent for now. "Because of this, I would travel, give lectures and interviews, and meet interesting, engaged people. At the same time, I would have a loving, healthy relationship with a man who shared my concerns, along with my interests in art, literature, music, and history. I would also have my happy family and a wide circle of friends to enjoy and grow with."

This time, I put my pen down with such a sigh that Chris could hear me in the open kitchen beyond the dividing counter. He was back at my side in seconds.

"Hmmm," he said, after reading my short fantasy blurb. "You aren't asking for the world. This is certainly doable. Just keep it in your head, as we continue to work—and visualize it whenever you can. Imprint it in your mind. Vibrate it. Let people know it's what you deserve. Let yourself know. Truly. Because I don't think you quite realize that you do—yet."

"No," I looked at him gloomily. "I don't think I do."

But I could feel hope pushing its courageous way to the top.

After lunch, I took the train to the pretty, riverside town of Richmond, where Lori picked me up in her car at the busy station. Because she had been such a loyal ally from the beginning of my stay in the UK, she and her family were most definitely on my farewell list. I couldn't leave without one last, heart-warming visit.

In fact—I persuaded myself in my best rationalizing inner voice—the rest of the day was going to be too emotional to even attempt any RTH techniques. I would begin applying them some other time. Tomorrow, I promised.

Procrastination ruled.

Lori and I drove a few blocks to the sweeping lawns that led down to the Thames. We parked and went in search of a patio for a quick glass of cold lemonade in the unseasonably warm sun.

In towns like Richmond, I always found it hard to believe that such now-fashionable centres could have witnessed so much history over the centuries. When the Scottish rebel leader William Wallace—a.k.a. Mel Gibson in the film *Braveheart*—was executed in London in 1305, his allies rode down to this area from the Highlands to kneel before King Edward I and pledge their allegiance.

If I closed my eyes, I could almost picture them riding by on exhausted horses, hoping to make peace—and save their own necks. I was tempted to salute in recognition, just to be friendly.

Lori and I had planned to go biking from her home on the High Street in Hampton Hill. So after basking in the sun and catching up superficially on each other's lives, we hopped back into her car and followed the road as it wound through a series of colourful villages, considered to be London's southwestern suburbs.

Names like Twickenham and Teddington whizzed by.

I was always impressed by the way my fellow Canadian manoeuvred so fearlessly—on the wrong side for us—between approaching and parked cars along those narrow roadways. Very quietly, I counted backwards from one hundred as we squeezed through what looked to be impossible spaces at high speeds. But she too had earned my confidence. I trusted her driving memes.

Once in Lori's backyard, we grabbed a couple of bicycles, threw some water bottles (not plastic) in the quaint little baskets attached to the handlebars, and crossed the street to Bushy Park, the second largest of London's royal parks.

I loved this place because of the herds of deer roaming freely among the trees and bushes. In spite of their rather pointed antlers, they mingled unthreateningly with mothers pushing carriages, cricket players, and cyclists. And every once in a while you could see one standing on its hind legs reaching for a particularly tender leaf above.

What made these creatures all the more fascinating was that they were first installed by that cranky Henry VIII of the many wives, who loved hunting when he wasn't seducing, marrying, divorcing, or executing. There were also signs that the area had been settled as far back as the Bronze Age, four thousand years ago, making Henry seem like a recent resident.

(To say nothing of our presence.)

Lori and I decided to cycle across the park to Hampton Court Palace, which Henry VIII took over from his once-favourite Cardinal Wolsey in 1529 and expanded to match his obviously inflated ego. We followed what were sometimes barely visible paths across fields, through woods, and over an arching bridge until we came to the Lion Gate entrance of the palace.

Like Kensington Palace, the gate and some of the landscaping owed their design to that hyperactive fellow, Christopher Wren. The pink brick Hampton Court was once expected to rival Louis

XIV's sumptuous Versailles, but it never quite reached that level of French decadence. That might be because British kings were too worried about losing their heads, as Charles I already had by that period.

And Louis XVI would eventually.

But Lori and I weren't really there as tourists. We simply wanted to appreciate the gardens and the riverbank—and talk. We climbed off our bikes, found a nice, shaded spot by the water, and made ourselves comfortable. Feeling wonderfully content, I started soaking up the combination of centuries of human creativity and quiet, unassuming nature—but didn't have very long before Lori began speaking about more serious matters than we had in Richmond.

"So where do things stand with Julian these days?" she asked, knowing I would be more than eager to share the gruesome details. She had been a generous and wise confidante over the past months—often frustrated by my lack of, well, progress.

I told her that Julian and I had spent the previous afternoon together, and that he didn't want to see me again until it was time to drive to the airport.

"Bastard," she blurted.

This was a joke between us, not to be taken too seriously—although not altogether inaccurate. "I hope you plan *not* to contact him before then. You've never been very good at playing it cool, and maybe now is the time to start."

I promised I wouldn't go anywhere near Julian's email address or phone numbers, not even a text, but admitted it would be difficult. I was such a sap.

"Perhaps knowing that you're leaving for a long period will help concentrate his mind," Lori said optimistically. "He hasn't had to commit so far, but now he should realize the time has come."

I told her I didn't think he'd change his position in any way before I left in six short days. He seemed ready to accept my departure, tough as I knew it would be for him.

"It seems so sad," Lori said empathetically. "He obviously cares a lot about you, but just can't make the leap. You've got to try to get over him."

I mumbled something in agreement, which I knew she wouldn't believe. If only I was better armed with some of Chris's wisdom and could list off several impressive intentions. Lori would have been delighted to hear strong, determined words coming out of my mouth—but nothing did.

I was stuck—caught between my newly acquired awareness and my old, repetitious ways.

Lori's own experience hadn't always been easy since she had arrived in the UK ten years before. After meeting a handsome, younger Englishman on a beach in Costa Rica, she married him, had two darling children, and then left. It turned out that she and her holiday suitor weren't quite as compatible as they had thought.

But sensible, well-travelled Lori didn't let the green British grass grow under her feet. She was now living with an older—and sexy—man who had already raised two children of his own and was a responsible parent and provider. Although he did like his pub nights!

Because Lori was settled, I had greedily turned to her for advice. However, I was afraid she was getting a little tired of my not following up on her suggestions—to contact this individual or that organization, to attempt to get a work visa, to be a real person, basically.

So there I was, sitting on a bank of the Thames, waiting to head home as what I considered to be a dismal flop—in spite of Chris's exhortations to the contrary. I had realized too late that I should have followed Lori's advice.

Was I any better equipped to follow Chris's?

We rode our bikes back by a different, equally beautiful route in order to be on time to pick up Lori's children from their neighbourhood schools. When they saw me, their unofficial aunt, they ran excitedly toward us, gave me big, loud hugs, held my hand as we walked, and told me happy tales of their secure lives in Hampton Hill.

A couple of hours later, I wept as I left their home and saw their sweet faces in the window, hands waving wildly. Goodbye. Goodbye. See you someday.

***

There was little time to spend missing loved ones in those final, frantic days. Next, I was on my way to Charing Cross Tube Station to meet Leila, a friend I'd met at a fundraiser for an Indian charity.

Actually, my real destination was the hotel next door to the station, which I knew well. Too well. I was once stuck in a cubicle in its basement loo. As I struggled with the lock, I could picture myself standing on the toilet, shouting futilely for hours, as happy staff members and guests came and went in the lobby above. (No, I couldn't climb over or under the door or sides because they extended from floor to ceiling!)

When I finally broke free, feeling like an out-of-practice escape artist in the process, I made my way back to the lobby, trying to look as calm and collected as possible.

Ah, those bizarre little adventures, I thought as I approached Charing Cross. They were like skill-testing challenges on the never-ending obstacle course that had been my life. The problem was that I couldn't seem to get enough of them! I liked the cut and thrust of it all. The surprises. The thrills. Would I ever calm down and grow up?

Tomorrow, I promised once again.

Sorry, Chris.

With Leila, I never knew what to expect. That was one of the joys of this person, the daughter of a dignified, retired, British-businessman father and, from all accounts, a wild, spontaneous, even tempestuous, Iranian-immigrant mother. Therefore, Leila, with her untameable, long brown hair, had the accent of a gentrified lady and the soul of an itinerant poet. She did, in fact, paint and write poetry but also led

American tourists across England, Ireland, France, and Italy—her specialities. (I once called her mobile phone and she answered from the Vatican.) She also renovated houses—by herself.

She was the embodiment of eclectic. It was enjoyable to go with her flow.

"Kathleen, so wonderful to see you," Leila cried, as soon as we met in the hotel, "but we can't visit just yet. I'm on a mission and need your help. A jolly mission!"

She told me that she'd been filmed a few months earlier showing a Turkish television personality around London for a programme on Turks living in the city—and had just received an email that the show would be aired that evening.

"We need to find a place that picks up Turkish television. Fast!"

I rushed over to the reception desk to make enquiries while Leila texted a few people who might be able to help. Facing a handsome young man behind the counter, I confessed that I had an odd question to ask—and, as luck or the universe would have it, he turned out to be Turkish. I shouted excitedly to Leila, and we were soon on our way to Wood Green Tube Station in the Turkish section of the city, armed with the names of various restaurants blessed with Cable TV.

After finding a suitable spot, we told the restaurant owner the reason for our being there that evening and he kindly sat us at the table closest to the TV—not generally my dining location of choice. Once we had examined the menu, Leila and I ordered almost everything offered: a Greek-like salad, soft flatbread, liquid-yogurt drinks, eggplant stews on rice, and some sort of delicious pastry for dessert.

It all looked so tasty.

When I spied Leila's face on the screen above us, I leapt up with my camera to get a photo of the two Leilas—one in a diner in London and the other floating in TV land. I'm sure the surrounding patrons found the whole exercise quite amusing, as Leila smiled brightly, spreading her hands to indicate the feast before her, and I danced around snapping pictures.

It was a typical night with my exotic friend, who I knew I would miss terribly.

Like Lori, Leila had followed my travails with Julian and, like Lori, had advised me to run as far and fast as I could. When I told her that he wanted to drive me to the airport on Monday, she sighed and told me that it was a "beautiful but cruel" act. Typically, he was being kind but inevitably hurtful.

Nevertheless, Leila and I both knew I couldn't get on the plane without a long, tearful parting from this man who had meant so much to me while in the UK.

❧

I arrived home late, tired, but exhilarated and determined. My unconscious playtime with my friends was over! I simply *had* to start incorporating RTH tactics into my daily life.

"You'll just have to come back as soon as you can," said Chris, when I told him how difficult the day had been in some ways. How many people I would miss.

"Yes, yes, yes," I replied glumly, picturing my almost-empty bank account.

As an antidote, I suggested a pre-bedtime therapy session. Was there something I could do to help me come back down to earth? Something that would make me feel more empowered when I laid my weary head on the pillow in a short while?

"Well," Chris paused. "They say necessity is the Mother of Invention; perhaps it can inspire Self-Reinvention! Are you sure you're up for it?"

A few more pleas on my part and I was soon at the dining table with my usual therapeutic weapons: pen and paper. Chris had suggested I try to look deeply and seriously at **What Is in My Behaviour/My Attitude That Prevents Me from Achieving My Goals/Stretching Myself**. (Had he been following me all afternoon and evening, taking notes as I postponed applying his wisdom?)

He put his nose back into the book he had been reading.

I rested my chin on one hand and tried to concentrate on the task before me. I knew that both Lori and Leila along with other dear friends—even Julian—had great faith in my energy and abilities, so why couldn't I deliver on my own promise? What were the barriers? Why was I there at the RTH in such a state of confusion? Lost...

After what seemed an eternity of fiddling with my pen, I wrote, "If I look deep down, there is a negative attitude insisting that 'poor little me' doesn't deserve success, security, and respect. The fact is I don't identify with them. I identify with losing, rather than winning. I can't picture myself as a stable, fully confident adult.

"Instead, I'm just a wandering, happy-go-lucky child—at least on the outside. I'm motivated to a certain extent but seem to sabotage any real success or gain. It's always start/stop/start, both professionally and personally."

I dropped my pen on the table and heard Chris jump slightly in his chair behind me. I really had been putting his nerves to the test! I turned and handed him the paper.

"This sounds pretty bleak, but I think it's quite accurate," I said.

We were getting into the deep stuff now. My life coach was slowly, but surely putting chinks in my solidly constructed armour. Freud could not have worked his magic with greater dexterity.

After a long few minutes, as Chris read and I twitched nervously, he turned to me.

"It's worth reiterating what I said earlier about negative memes. The main reason why you have a negative attitude toward yourself—thinking you don't deserve success, security, respect, and so on—is that you have a deeply ingrained thinking habit or meme of negative analysis. This makes you tell yourself that you've failed or done something wrong over and over again."

He flapped the page he was holding back and forth, as if it had suddenly become hot in the room.

"This negative-analysis habit is *not* your fault. It's one of the main environmental factors that all of us in the Western, so-called developed world have to face from childhood. If a child is constantly given—or hears others being given—negative feedback at an early stage in her life, she'll automatically and unconsciously pick it up as a major part of her thinking process. We all do."

"I resemble that statement, as my brother says," I sighed. Chris smiled at me sympathetically, but it was clear he had more to add to his theory.

"Thinking or learning how to think is one of the main developmental processes of every human being. If you were unlucky and brought up in a household or community where your role models—parents, siblings, relatives, teachers—were regularly concentrating on what's *wrong* with the world and each other or why you and others are useless, ineffective, naughty, etc., you automatically learn to think this way yourself.

"It's important to remember that, if this negativity happens in your immediate environment five, ten, or fifty times a day, it will total fifty-thousand to five-hundred-thousand times over the first twenty years. You can't help but become bloody good at it. Anybody who repeats any behaviour five-hundred-thousand times is bound to become an expert!"

"No wonder the word 'programming' keeps popping up," I agreed. It did seem as though our young minds were terribly vulnerable to all sorts of suggestions—too many of them damaging.

"You should be aware too that because you, Kathleen, are a quick, intelligent, sensitive thinker, you absorbed these thinking habits faster and more thoroughly than many people. In other words, your intelligence has contributed to your problems."

My intelligence was a handicap? How horrible was that? Before I could react as pessimistically as Chris knew I might, he ploughed ahead.

"It can also contribute to your solutions. You're intelligent enough to turn this around by rearranging your mental outlook, so that you get loads of positive-thinking practice. If you do a 3,2,1 Reviewing analysis, which we discussed last night, five times a day for a month, you'll quickly become very good at it.

"Or when you get home, you can start identifying your daughter's skills, strengths, and qualities, for example. You could give yourself a target of one every day for a month, explaining their importance to her. She's relatively young and starting out in life, so she needs every bit of positive/success feedback she can get. Like everyone else, she's probably had more than her fair share of negative/failure exposure."

"You try to protect them when they're young and innocent, but it's virtually impossible—especially, I guess, when you're damaged yourself," I noted. "Although my daughter is tremendously positive. *She* could give lessons!"

Chris nodded. "The more you do these exercises with your daughter, your mother, your siblings, your friends—in fact, with everybody you come across—the more practice you'll get and the more skilled you become at looking on the bright side. Life gets better and better!"

"You make it sound like such a fulfilling route to follow." I was feeling genuinely heartened by his words.

Chris leaned toward me earnestly. "If you can get people to realize that they have a whole raft of real, not imaginary, skills, strengths, and qualities available and that they can pick and choose how to use them to help themselves and others, then they'll automatically flourish and develop as strong, motivated, contributing members of society."

"What a thought to end the day." I felt almost as breathless as Chris appeared to be. He certainly did love life coaching—and rightly so.

"Yes, it's best to go out with a bang," Chris agreed. Then he gave me what could only be described as a sheepish grin. "You probably won't want to do this now, but I have another exercise that I think will help you immensely. I'd like you to begin thinking about the Necessary Developments Within Yourself That Would Contribute to Your Becoming an Ideal Human Being.

"Why don't you let your unconscious mind work on this during the night? That's always a good time to formulate new ideas and concepts, especially if you programme your mind before you go to sleep, plant some seeds, as you close your eyes. You aren't actually thinking because that requires the conscious mind, but impressive things can be accomplished while pounding the pillow."

Within half an hour, I was doing just that, despite my exhaustion. These pre-departure days were not only full to the hilt but also emotionally, spiritually, and intellectually challenging—and draining.

No problem there! I wouldn't have changed anything, except having Julian at my side more often.

"Now," I asked myself as I drifted off, "what are the Necessary Developments Within Myself That Would Contribu . . . ?"

CHAPTER ELEVEN

Bring You Peace

❧

Nothing can bring you peace but yourself.
—Ralph Waldo Emerson, *Self-Reliance*

I woke up the next morning, Day 10—but who was counting?—with my head full of urgent messages. Chris's suggestion about before-bed fertilizing of the mind had been very helpful, not that that should come as any surprise. His quietly dispensed wisdom always hit the bull's eye—at least in the case of this particular target.

So, I thought, I have to list the **Necessary Developments Within Myself That Would Contribute to My Becoming an Ideal Human Being.** Ideal? That was a stretch. Then again, I was there at the RTH to do exactly that. Stretch. The "Ideal" part might take longer.

Because of the work my brain had already done during the night, the usual white piece of paper didn't seem quite so glaringly empty when I placed it on the duvet cover in front of me. Yes, I was staying in bed. Chris had suggested that he serve me breakfast there to allow me to work without any other worries. I was propped up on my feather pillows feeling like, well, like an Ideal Human Being—or on my way!

I began to write:

"I need a better self-image—that of a confident, capable woman, not of a lost girl." (Julian had told me I needed to grow up, but just by a few years.)

"I need to heal my inner wounds, truly deal with them, and be whole." (The peace and serenity of mindfulness meditation had begun to help with this. I had to get back to it.)

"I must continue to become more aware of what or who is really me, not fantasies, misconceptions, half-truths, and programming." (Figure out which memes are harmful and get rid of them. Keep only what helps.)

"I need to be as conscious as possible of my thoughts and actions, and pay close attention to what comes up from my unconscious mind—where the demons lie."

"I need to broaden my sense of myself and my options. I won't have choices unless I realize they are there."

"I need to develop clearer goals and visualize the heck out of them." (They *will* be achieved!)

"I must learn how to focus/concentrate my efforts and energies."

"I should/must earn/expect respect."

"I need to go beyond myself and relate to the concerns and problems of others—and offer to help, if I can."

"I need to understand more, worry less."

"Ready for your kippers?" came Chris's voice from the hall after several minutes—or hours.

My happy "Yes!" rang in my ears, sounding more like an infant in a high chair wearing a bib—an even younger comparison this time—than a grown woman. Obviously, I had work to do along the maturity line! On the other hand, I was determined to *enjoy* the long-overdue process of becoming more adult.

The word "incorrigible" flashed in my head while I handed Chris my latest list and reached for my brekkie—breakfast.

But there were grounds for hope, I told myself. Major transformation *was* possible. The proof? Who would have thought I would develop a taste for kippers first thing in the day? To my mind, this clearly demonstrated beyond a shadow of a doubt that I and my problems weren't immutable.

Anything could happen!

※

Later, downstairs, as I sat in a more serious teaching arrangement across the table from Chris, he asked if I could recall the paragraph I had written when I described who I was to a stranger on the train. He slid the piece of paper with my scribbled words over to me.

"This, along with what you wrote earlier this morning, makes it very clear that we need to develop a precise plan of action. Yesterday, you wrote that you 'can't seem to focus' and aren't 'grounded.' You're 'scattered' and 'merely trying to survive.' Today you wrote about needing a better 'self-image' and 'healing wounds.' You want to 'broaden' your sense of yourself and 'develop clearer goals.'"

He was silent for a moment, as if gathering his energy for the challenge ahead. "First of all, I tend to believe that the more progress you see yourself making in the present, the less relevant the ghosts of the past will be. It will also begin to heal those wounds—or, at least, make them less relevant.

"Also, you mention 'respect.' Once you see yourself doing what *you* want to be doing, the happier and more respectful you will be toward You. That's the most important thing of all. The basis of everything else."

"The word respect always seems to spring up," I agreed. "I suppose self-respect is the obvious starting point."

"I think your main stumbling block is that you've had a fair amount of success and positive feedback during the past six months—during your entire life, in fact—but it hasn't satisfied your own specific criteria. This is absolutely crucial. You can never fool yourself. You have your own standards and expectations, even if they're unexpressed, and, if you don't live up to them, you just can't win. That's why you have to know and articulate Who You Are as well as possible, which you've made a good start at."

"A good start?" I asked, causing Chris to raise his eyebrows slightly. Was that all? Then again, who was I kidding? I was a beginner, taking my first steps to change and self-realization. This was an ongoing process that would probably take me years . . . forever . . .

"So now I'd like you to write down the **Top Five Characteristics of an Ideal Job or Activity.**"

He handed me the page I had been writing on in bed about the Necessary Developments Within Myself and so on. That wish list was all well and good—great intentions—but it appeared that for this next exercise I had to be proactive and specific, rather than introspective and abstract (with a typical dash of self-pity).

This would be much more difficult. What Job or Activity did I want? What? What? What? It really was time I asked myself that question—and came up with a sound answer, one I could live *with* and *by*. Why hadn't the Jobs and Activities of my past been satisfactory, a good match?

I wrote down, "Dealing with ideas. Intellectual." I needed some kind of satisfaction for my mind or I got bored and frustrated—which had happened fairly regularly in the past. Then, "Helping people. Changing the world." I couldn't ignore the bad state of the planet. I had to be engaged in some way, working to solve one or more of its many problems, improving conditions for my daughter and others—before it was too late.

What else? "Communication. Interacting with people." As I've mentioned, I am a social creature. It's inter-act—not Internet—or wither up for me. Good, solid, face-to-face engaging, although I did like to interface in the realm of the virtual, too. I couldn't survive without email! (No online dating so far, though.)

"Travelling—the non-virtual kind." That was key. I loved to immerse myself in different languages and cultures, which were surprisingly vibrant in this age of corporate globalization—in spite of the cookie-cutter sameness creeping in everywhere.

Fast foods. Wal-Mart. Disney.

"Being creative." I couldn't be a cog in a wheel. There were impulses within me that needed to be dealt with, needed an artistic channel of escape. Oh, and one more, "Treated with respect." That persistent word—self and otherwise. I wasn't sure why it was so essential, really. Not many people are treated with respect in this world.

Was I being too demanding? Asking the impossible?

"Right," said Chris, after glancing at my words. That was all. He reached for the printed list, entitled Characteristics of an Ideal Human Being, on which I had rated my own characteristics earlier in the week.

"Now, you gave characteristics such as purposeful, ambitious, and motivated your lowest grades the other night. That's not the end of the story. There are no dead ends. I believe that every problem or obstacle provides an opportunity.

"Remember how we turned your failures into Positive Objectives, not long after you arrived? Your failure to do something was transformed into your determination to do it?" I nodded. "We also touched on the idea that weaknesses are actually strengths that have been mistimed or misapplied. Do you think you can list the **Main Opportunities Your Weaker Characteristics Might Present You**? This is similar and just as critical, perhaps more so. I'm not saying it will be easy."

I stared blankly at Chris. Failures as objectives, I could understand; weaknesses as badly timed or badly applied strengths sounded good too—in a vague sort of way. But weaknesses as actual Opportunities? Was he kidding? Failures were something you *didn't* do, but weaknesses were something you *couldn't* do.

Big difference.

The look on Chris's face showed that he certainly was not kidding. No such luck! I was on the hot seat and I had to deliver.

For some reason, this exercise was the most difficult so far! It meant that all those Weaker Characteristics, which I had been beating myself up over, might not be as all-powerful as I had always thought.

They could somehow be overcome or transformed into oblivion—as Opportunities.

But they were *my* weaknesses, I protested silently. Part of my identity. How could I simply neutralize or reverse them? I had been using them to undermine my progress for years, telling myself I lacked purpose, I was unambitious, unmotivated, and so on. In some warped way, I relied on them. They were my protection, my cover.

"Would you prefer to cling to your Weaker Characteristics, Kathleen?" Chris asked gently, interrupting the silence that sat heavily on the table between us. "Many people do. It's much easier to stick with old, well-worn habits, rather than parking them and adopting new, unfamiliar ones—even if they're healthier and more productive."

I pushed my chair back, stood up, and began to prowl around the small crowded room—not an easy space for such aggressive activity. In fact, I almost bumped into one of the bookshelves. I felt like a caged animal, although the bars that were hemming me in were invisible.

After all these RTH exercises, which I had been treating with a certain amount of levity over the past few days, Chris had finally managed to cut deep into my psyche, my personality, my being. I couldn't believe how affected I was by the prospect of releasing myself from my own self-image prison.

I sat down on the bottom step of the staircase, and glared at Chris. "I don't know what to say," I confessed. "If I get rid of my weaknesses, my excuses, I will have to be a real person. Don't you understand? I'm not sure I can handle that! You're pushing me out of the nest, or some other silly analogy, and expecting me to flap my wings and fly."

Chris looked at me for several endless seconds. His eyes, deep, almost bottomless, met mine.

"You came here because the nest wasn't working for you. You needed more. You hoped to start flying. Remember? It's what you wanted. What you still want. You have to believe that. Don't turn back now even though you have a fear of heights."

I bowed my head in order to avoid his gaze. Of course, he was right. I couldn't, shouldn't, and didn't want to turn back. I was, to continue the analogy, ready to flap my wings and enjoy the freedom, the fresh air, even the sheer drop below me. Ready to soar. Come on, I urged myself, let's go—and let go. Throw away all those negative safety mechanisms! Now!

I stood up, walked back to the table, and sat down. "Okay, how do I do this?"

Chris spoke strongly but calmly like a doctor dealing with a frightened patient who has just leapt off the examining table and darted for the door, hospital gown flapping open, revealing all.

"Well, let's start with 'purposeful.' You say you aren't very. I disagree. To my mind, you're extremely purposeful most of the time—and saying that you aren't simply isn't accurate."

He pressed on. "It's only when it comes to finding a purpose for your life as a whole, establishing what your life is for, and why you are living that you find difficult. Of course, that's why we're doing these exercises."

I told him that I sensed that my life was nothing more than a series of events—albeit many of them amusing and exciting. There didn't seem to be any game plan. Instead of building something definite, I was reacting to various apparently arbitrary happenings, always having to start fresh—new job, new home, new man, and so on.

Chris persisted. "You say you're 'reacting to various apparently arbitrary happenings.' To me, that comment reflects one of your main obstacles: seeing your strengths as weaknesses, and, therefore, dead ends rather than Opportunities. You have an inquisitive mind that's constantly looking for and responding to interesting matters and events—just like most successful scientists, psychologists, explorers, and journalists, among others.

"If they see something that puzzles or interests them, they latch onto it and go wherever it takes them. You have exactly this sort of instinct and drive." He hesitated. "But in your case, you lack a clear objective to give this instinct/drive some context—to guide you as a journalist, for example, into following the right story and asking the appropriate searching questions.

"If you had a mission to expose some critical issue, such as corporate corruption undermining our societies, you could begin to research various leads, and contact activists, politicians, honest business people, and others who share your concern. You could help expose the bad apples—at least, some of them."

Another longer hesitation. "Having a clear plan or objective guides your thought processes, your observations, and your actions. It gives you purpose."

"I can see where that would make a big difference," I noted. "It would allow a person to build in a more systematic way, instead of being so haphazard and hit-or-miss."

"This is why I believe that weaknesses and strengths are two sides of the same coin. The perceived weakness of 'reacting to various apparently arbitrary happenings' is in fact a strength, when applied to something concrete. It's an Opportunity, if you exploit it properly.

"But—and there are always buts—if you're going to make sense of all this, you have to define your main, long-term goals. Within that context, you need to practise setting yourself coherent, short-term objectives and write down a statement in response to the questions: What do I want to achieve in journalism—or another field—in the next six months? What outcomes am I aiming for?

"You need to become more focussed and specific professionally." With a sweep of his hand, he added, "And let the home and the man come along in the wake of the job."

"Right," I responded somewhat cynically. 'But planning of any sort is new for me."

"After lunch, why don't you write down on that dreaded piece of paper Three Main Occupations/Professional Activities You Would Most Like to Pursue for the Rest of Your Life—what you could do that would make a real difference. You mentioned them in passing when you described Your Ideal Life, I believe, but they're worth repeating. Remember, by aiming high, you will probably succeed. By aiming low or not aiming at all, you're guaranteed little or nothing."

"Too true," was all I could say.

Chris had finally narrowed our search down to the basic flaw, and, as they say, it wasn't pretty. I had simply not taken the time or effort to come up with a plan of action—productive action. Instead, I had manoeuvred my way round and round in circles like a ballet dancer who hadn't learned the next steps, and just kept twirling.

It was dizzying.

When we stopped for our break, I realized I was feeling quite weak. All this redirecting took a lot out of me. No wonder so few people were able to do it on their own. It really did require major hand-holding and guidance—unless you were a very determined, inner-driven human being. But if you were like that, you probably wouldn't be suffering from muddled angst in the first place!

On the contrary, I knew that millions were in the same situation as I was. Needing a boost. A hand. I certainly wasn't alone. I had lots and lots of frustrated company. The difference was that I'd found Chris. Or he'd found me. Or was it that wise, old universe again?

Our tasty, organic salads downed, it was back to work. I picked up our dishes and took them to the kitchen, following Chris's strict instructions *not* to wash them. He was quite aware that I had plans for the late afternoon and evening and he was determined to squeeze every second's worth of improvement time out of me . . . us.

"As I said earlier, before you write down your short-term objectives, which are pivotal, I'd like you to list **Three Main Occupations/Professional Activities You Would Most Like to Pursue for the Rest of Your Life.**"

"Oh God, do I really have to articulate them with such certainty? Pin myself down? Be that definite and clear?" I heard myself bellyaching. "Right. Right. I'll do it," I added quickly. "Yes. Yes. Great idea."

I now sounded like I was stalling for time. I guess I was. It was a major step to genuinely commit to future actions, rather than dreaming about them.

Chris walked toward the kitchen. "I'm going to do the dishes," he called over his shoulder. "We'll both be working, although I know your job is much more difficult than mine. Especially the commitment part!"

"I want to write a book that will change people's lives," I called back. "That's Number One."

"Write it down," Chris responded, turning on the taps and drowning out any further conversation.

"I want to improve my journalism," I scribbled. I hadn't been putting any real effort into it lately—my columns were becoming increasingly fluffy—and I was certainly beginning to appreciate the value and necessity of genuine, unfettered effort. That and a positive attitude seemed an unbeatable combination.

"I want to get more involved in improving the world with something substantial to say, and take part in everything from real-life conferences to blogs and Twitter. Maybe even YouTube!"

There were so many ideas in my head with nowhere to go. My columns had given me one medium, but they seemed to disappear into thin air. If and when they were published, I rarely saw any of the Letters to the Editor in response. The feedback. Besides, the newspaper business was faltering fast, sadly, as my friend Nick had explained in his book.

But there were exciting new media, which people were using to get and stay in touch, be engaged—and I wanted to participate in them. I was tired of being ineffectual.

"The dishes are done," said a voice beside me. "How are you doing? Was it as difficult as you thought it would be?"

"No, it wasn't," I stated. "I guess I have more of a plan in my head than I realized. All this running around declaring I don't know what or who I am and I *do*—to some extent."

"Now, now," Chris chastised me patiently. "Stop that negative thinking. Self-doubt. It's your worst enemy. Send it running. Every bit of it. You've just written down three achievable goals. Now why don't you take the first one and write **Three Main Reasons Why You Want to Write a Book**. You want to write this book, but to what ends?"

I wrote "Three Main Reasons" just below my first list.

It was a strange feeling to inform myself of what I was actually thinking and wanting. We all have so many random, disorganized thoughts and dreams in our heads. Gathering them together and articulating them was a bit like herding cats—or those naughty puppies I mentioned earlier.

Reason One: "Perhaps I'm being selfish (ooops, negative), but I love writing and putting thoughts down on paper—or the computer. It's creative and satisfying bringing impressions and experiences together in an original way."

Reason Two: "I want my book to act as a springboard for my being more effective socially and politically. External change. I would like to use it to find people and organizations who feel as I do—and work with them to rebuild our democracies, narrow the widening gap between the rich and poor, and more. Somehow, they're all related."

Reason Three: "I want to take whatever I've learned from Chris and send it out into the world to help other people with their lives. Internal change. I want to be able to offer meaningful guidance. I hate being lost and I know others do, too."

Chris picked up my latest declarations. "I know you have to go soon, so I'll just say one more thing. Take what you've written here and get on with it! Right?"

I cringed slightly but noticeably, I was sure. (I had been doing a lot of that over the past week or more.) Why did anything that sounded like a commitment make me feel so nervous and claustrophobic? What prevented me from doing exactly what I wanted to do, especially now that I knew what it was—and there was no reason not to?

My dreams and desires were no longer a vague blur in my unconscious mind. They were there in black and white. But old habits, memes, and safety mechanisms die hard. Somehow, I had to move the many words I had written at the RTH off the page and into my daily life.

Would I or could I do it?

"Thank you so very much, Chris," I said, standing up and walking around the table. "You have no idea how much all of this helps." I gave him a hug, trying to be as casual as possible.

"Actually, I do!" he said, as I withdrew my arms and began to walk away.

The rest of my day was packed from the moment I left the RTH. First, in central London, I was joining two friends, Barbara and Joan, whom I had met not long after my arrival. Later, I would be dashing north to my old stomping grounds to attend a dinner party and lecture.

Unlike Lori and Leila, both younger than I was, Barbara and Joan were older professionals. They weren't necessarily wiser than their younger counterparts, but they were more *seasoned*. They could judge life and people based on their own lengthier observations.

I decided that this would be a good time to put Chris's techniques into action, specifically Plan, Act, Review, Improve (PARI). Plan: I would be as focussed and upbeat as I possibly could; no more indulging in futile self-pity.

Barbara, a successful lawyer who was also relatively new to London, had suggested we join Joan for a farewell afternoon tea in a boutique hotel near Kensington Palace. It sounded perfect for a final outing. You can't have too much tea in the UK.

And you can't have too much Palace.

When I arrived at the hotel, I couldn't believe the coincidence. It was the same gorgeous place Simone and I had been admiring from the outside, as we had made our way to the underground just one week earlier. We had even peeked like inquisitive children through the small leaded windows at the chintz-and-flower-filled tea room on the ground floor—and I had told Simone how much I would love to sink into all that cushy elegance.

Now I was about to!

From the instant I walked into the lobby, I felt terribly upper crust. All I was missing was one of those bright, decorative hats which are still worn in some circles in the UK—the kind I hadn't owned since attending Sunday school as a child. Mine even had ribbons down the back that I was extremely proud of.

My friends hadn't arrived yet, but a neatly uniformed waiter led me into the tea room. Thinking I would leave the choice of a table to the group, I sat down to wait on an ornate loveseat with adorable throw cushions. Its tasteful decadence made me want to sprawl across it, head back with a cigarette holder between my lips, silk-stockinged legs crossed.

Dahlings, I could drawl when they entered. How absolutely diviiine to see you! You're both looking simply faaabulous!

Within minutes, Barbara and Joan joined me—I offered them a simple hello and hugs—and we picked a table beside a window overlooking Kensington Gardens. Not far from the grand piano. Good start.

We were soon presented with a menu of the various teas available, which was a little daunting. I have mixed feelings about menus with words I can't quite pronounce. They tempt you to try new things—but it's intimidating to actually ask for them.

Mispronunciation, stumbling, and apologizing are almost inevitable.

Not wanting to walk on the wild side in such a haute environment or enjoy a powerful caffeine hit so late in the day, I ordered a sweetly scented, loose-leaf jasmine; Barbara went traditional with Earl Grey, and Joan chose a Darjeeling. We then ordered a round of scones, clotted cream, and jams, which are *de rigueur* in such places.

Any thought of waistlines or thighs was forbidden—or impossible, we joked.

Two hours later, bloated and full of cheer, we decided to wrap up our farewell event. It had been entertaining and enlightening, as we each summed up our lives to date. I'd mentioned Julian only briefly, casually telling my chums that he would be taking me to the airport—and the exasperated looks on their faces was all I needed to understand their positions on the matter.

"It might be good to put some distance between the two of you," said Joan, a doctor and mother of four. "That should tell the tale, if you know what I mean."

I knew.

With this, my superconscious mind screamed inside my skull, advising me that it was time to Act. "Yes, I think it will be helpful for me to get away and start living life on my own terms," I stated matter-of-factly. There was a satisfying look of surprise on my friends' faces. It wasn't what they were used to hearing from me.

Such strength and determination!

"You sound better about this than usual," Barbara said. "Have you been doing some serious soul-searching? Taking assertiveness training? Whatever your secret, bottle it!"

I sat back to Review my own words—and the reaction to them—with a kind of Cheshire Cat grin on my face. I hadn't said anything about the RTH, not wanting to get into the complex details, but I concluded that I had just passed a crucial test with two savvy women. My first real step toward systematic attitude and image transformation.

As for Improve, I simply told myself I had to do this more often!

After Joan left to pick up a child or two from school, Barbara informed me that she was very close to quitting her job at a prestigious university. She wasn't happy at all with her colleagues and desperately needed a change.

"Well, be careful," I advised. "Make sure you have something else to go to. You don't want to end up like me."

"I certainly don't," she agreed too quickly.

Fortunately, she had been such a good pal during my time in London, suggesting outings to the theatre and films, that I could only interpret her remark as completely honest, rather than cruel. But, coming right on the heels of my small PARI victory, it was a brutal reminder of how much work lay ahead. Somehow, I had ended up being the person whose life, even with its many upsides, was an example of what *not* to do.

That hurt.

As we prepared to leave, I was dying to tell Barbara that I was in the midst of turning my weaknesses into strengths, even opportunities, but decided to keep mum. It was impossible to sum up the RTH experience in a few short sentences.

Better to forge ahead without too much fanfare.

My next stop was the home of friends and former neighbours in Hampstead. They ran a charitable foundation from their attractive townhouse, which was large enough to handle dynamic, vegetarian dinner parties for up to sixty people. There was always a certain amount of elbow-bumping, but everyone enjoyed the compulsory closeness.

After the meal, our hosts led us half a block down the street to a large Georgian mansion that had been converted into an art gallery/meeting place, which regularly featured talks by guest speakers from around the world.

That night, the feisty Indian physicist Vandana Shiva spoke about protecting the biodiversity of the planet. She warned that large corporations were trying to take over and control the world's seed supply and that many varieties of plants had already disappeared—along with our food options.

It was an issue we knew we shouldn't ignore in spite of our comfortable lives—where all we had to do was head to a well-stocked supermarket for groceries.

Even this convenience lost its appeal when the post-lecture question and answer session focussed on the dwindling quality of most Western food, which is sometimes genetically modified, usually grown in dead soil, fertilized, sprayed, processed, packaged, shipped long distances, and more. Someone recommended becoming a locavore—eating local food, preferably organic—and most of us were ready to convert then and there.

In the midst of such honourable intentions, I thought of the flour—which had probably not been milled from regional wheat—in those delightful scones I'd enjoyed that afternoon. And it was highly unlikely that our tea leaves had been lovingly cultivated in some nearby garden!

Humbled by the challenges looming in yet another aspect of my existence, I joined the group for the pleasant walk back to my friends' home to enjoy more wine (non-local) and deeper conversation.

I didn't return to the RTH until very late that night.

It had been a long, winding, and wondrous day during which Chris had pushed me to the psychic and emotional wall; pushed me closer to recognizing myself—and my potential future. Also, I had successfully put into practice my first Sub-Personality Management exercise.

I could only hope that some of what I had learned and discovered would really stick in my brain and influence me.

The jury was still out.

CHAPTER TWELVE

Never Too Late

※

It's never too late to be what you might have been.
—George Eliot

It was much too early Friday morning, and we were already on the train heading north from King's Cross Station—a little later than scheduled. I wasn't complaining. Chris and I had managed to find four empty seats with a table and had settled in by the wide window, facing each other. There were books and picnic fixings spread out beside us.

It was going to be a four-plus-hour journey to Edinburgh, where we would switch to another line, and we hoped our little nest would remain ours for the duration. After all, we had work to do as we whizzed across England and into the eastern part of Scotland.

However, I was finding it an effort to be bright and alert in those waking hours because I had had a totally delightful Thursday, my last full day in London—for now.

First, I had met a pompous but entertaining friend for lunch near Regent's Park; then I'd rushed to a small pub not far from Piccadilly Circus to share some tales with a journalist pal, who, wisely, had managed to become an expert on the glories of Tuscany. (Travelling back and forth between the UK and Italy, he probably had the best commute of any working stiff on the planet!)

After that, I made my way to the City for a final rowdy chat and drinks with my dear buddy Bill. It was there that I decided to remodel myself in his eyes—and mine—just before we parted.

"I'm thinking of writing a book about my adventures in London," I told him with as much confidence in my voice as I could muster.

"Will it be a kiss and tell?" he joked, but I could sense genuine curiosity.

"No," I said, trying to remain in control. "I've learned a lot about myself and the world while I've been here, and I believe it would make interesting reading for others."

Goodness, I sounded stuffy. He must have been wondering what had got into me.

"Kathleen, I have complete and utter faith in you. Just make sure you send me a signed copy."

That was that. We soon returned to being our usual jolly selves, but I felt proud to have the endorsement of this dynamic, generous man who had done so much to make my longer stay possible. Providing a roof over the head of a virtual stranger was no empty gesture!

Finally, I took the tube to a home in legendary Bloomsbury for a noisy and stimulating dinner party with several of my fellow "guru shoppers," including Fiona, around a table—a round table, fortunately. That made it all the better for uninhibited and uninterrupted interaction.

In other words, the conversation was chaotic! It was survival of the fittest, as several people tried to be heard at once. With the words and wit flying, I didn't mention Chris and the RTH. Where or how would I begin?

"Excuse me, could everyone be quiet for a moment? I want to announce that I'm now undergoing an extreme personality and attitude makeover. Any questions or comments?" Don't think so.

I got back to Wimbledon at such a late hour that I thought I would never be able to rise on time for the train the next morning. But I did! And there I was, hazily eager to listen to my life coach once again, as England flashed before me.

My pre-exile therapy time was so running out.

Our rail destination was a small fishing village called Stonehaven, south of Aberdeen and just a few miles from the more inland Drumtochty Castle wedding site. We would spend the night in a small bed and breakfast before being met and driven to the wedding early afternoon Saturday. Then we would overnight in the castle itself!

Never having slept in a castle before, this aspect of the plan was my favourite. I was ready and willing to face the risk that some evil villain might decide to lock me up in a dungeon, keeping me prisoner as I spun gold thread until a prince . . .

Ah, the fantasies—and memes—of youth.

Back to modern reality. Since it was definitely breakfast time, Chris and I pulled out our muffins and coffee and laid them on the table. As we ate and drank, London's suburbs began to disappear and the greener countryside took their place. I loved looking out over the tidy fields and hills of this land, so familiar from all my favourite novels and films.

More memes.

Although we weren't crossing Jane Austen territory, which was mainly in the county of Hampshire along the south coast, the region we were passing through had a similar look and feel. There were cottages covered with rambling, mauve wisteria, rose gardens—their owners' pride and joy—and narrow, winding roads. I could almost picture Lizzie Bennet and Darcy, happily married, waving from a hilltop as we passed.

(Mega-memes! No wonder poor Ted from Kingston didn't stand a chance.)

Less romantically, I knew first-hand that those shoulderless roads were picturesque but not much fun for pedestrians. On a trip to the lovely county of Devon, I had had some close calls while trying to walk from one village to another—and more than once was tempted to dive headfirst into a hedge or ditch when cars came my way. Some things are preferable on postcards.

"Shall we get started?" Chris asked finally, breaking my reveries, as he put the plastic lid back on his coffee cup. "I know you're still gearing up for the day, but I'm going to do most of the talking at first, so why don't you just relax, continue eating, and listen. Of course, feel very free to ask questions or make comments at any time. We've got several hours on our hands."

"Terrific," I replied, with as much zeal as I could generate at that hour. "You did promise that this would also be a tourist venture, so I hope you won't mind if I interrupt now and then to ask you what we're passing. I'd hate to miss out on one of the joys of train travel: scenery."

"I completely agree," Chris grinned. "In fact, I'll interrupt myself, if I see anything of particular interest. Alright, during the time we have now, I want to fill in a few gaps in our chats over the past several days. I want to look a little more at your own meme-changing and then give you a few more tools you can use to deal with others. After all, you're heading home and will soon be immersed in family and friends, and, as we've discussed, there'll be some emotional baggage involved that won't be entirely positive."

I took a sip of coffee and shook my head slowly. In some ways, I didn't feel at all prepared to face certain people I had managed to avoid for several months. For that reason, one part of me would have liked to stay hidden away in the Scottish castle forever, while another, braver part wanted to face all those past dysfunctions as quickly as possible—post-RTH. I knew which one was healthier, but it was also the more demanding.

Was that a coincidence?

Probably not. Healthy actions and reactions always do take more effort—whether mental or physical, as I now knew too well.

It was so much easier to be a slug!

"Remember how we discussed the unconscious mind, which affects our behaviour patterns, our attitudes, and outlook?" Chris was asking, as I carefully rubbed my eyes and tried to focus. "Basically, I'm sure you'll recall, this is the part of our minds that you would describe as 'memetically driven.' It's programmed by life's experiences and lessons. There's no conscious thought involved."

"Yes, I'm becoming more and more cognizant of this aspect of my being," I sighed. "Its impact is both impressive and aggravating."

"Well, I think it's time to talk further about changing a few of the memes you've developed. More Sub-Personality Management, which I know you've been working on. As I told you a couple of days ago, ideally, memetic engineering isn't reprogramming in an inhuman, mechanical way. It's more thoughtful, intelligent, and active. *You* are in control, not some devious mindbender. It's all about total awareness—of yourself, those around you, and your society in general. Not a bad thing, right?"

"Count me in." I smiled, trying to ignore the woolly feeling in my head. Hangovers can do that, as I had found out too often in this fun-loving nation.

At the same time, there was something about the motion of the train that made me want to progress faster than ever. Perhaps all learning institutions should be placed on wheels, giving students a true feeling of advancement. I think I can. I think I can. Full steam ahead! By now, I could understand why Chris was so pleased about living beside the railway tracks.

Movement was what it was all about.

"For all of us," Chris continued, "information is constantly being fed into our brains—some for a very short period of time with no permanent impact, but most of it remains much longer, affecting us for the rest of our lives. So it's good to conduct a kind of **Internal Travelogue**, going to the different places in our brains to check out our meme flora and fauna. What's dwelling in there?"

This woke me up.

"'Internal Travelogue.' That sounds useful! It would be great to get up in the morning and do a quick examination of our programmed content—our flora and fauna, as you put it. We could even decide if there's anything that should be chucked out that day. 'I've got to get rid of my gossip meme,' we could tell ourselves over breakfast."

"It's not always quite that easy," Chris laughed, "but your idea is good. An Internal Travelogue usually entails repeating some of the self-awareness exercises we've been through, including reassessing how you rate yourself in terms of the Characteristics of an Ideal Human Being. Constant vigilance is what's needed! After all, if you don't watch over and control your memes, they will control you. Oh, we're about to pass Peterborough Cathedral, a stunning Norman creation, dating from the twelfth century. It's too bad we can't get closer."

We craned our necks, hoping for a glimpse.

"I think part of the problem is our modern society," Chris said, efficiently moving back from tour guide to mentor. "In earlier times, before everything was mechanized—when that cathedral was built, for example—humans dealt mainly with living beings. They *had* to recognize and nurture their own innate sensibilities and abilities, along with those in others.

"Now with industrialization and post-industrialization, we've become highly rational and scientific, and have lost touch with ourselves and those around us. We're so divorced from our own personal realities that we often act like the machines we depend on—being run on automatic pilot, surreptitiously by our memes. Programmed like robots.

"Most of those memes are buried deep within. The ones we have ready access to via our Internal Travelogue and can modify relatively easily are the tip of the iceberg. For this reason, as we've been doing with our exercises, we have to try to travel deeper and deeper, using a variety of routes and vehicles. It's necessary to keep trying over and over until there's some detectable change."

I thought of the RTH work I'd already done. How far had I gone beyond the iceberg tip?

"In other words," Chris continued, "we have to adopt the concept and practice of learning how to improve on a regular basis. It takes work, as you've seen. Repetitive, dedicated effort. This is the *only* way anyone can achieve what many call **Emotional Intelligence**."

"I read about that fairly recently," I said. "I like it. We're obsessed with our IQs, why not be obsessed with our EIQs? I would think the first isn't very worthwhile without the second when it comes to functioning in life."

"I would agree," Chris said. "There are several methods that can help a person increase his or her EIQ and move toward being an effective, competent friend, partner, or professional. One is called **Trial and Success Learning**. Success shows us what works in life and what to do, so we should take more advantage of it, analyze it, and learn from it. Of course, we should also try to learn from our failures, as you did earlier in our time together by turning them into Positive Objectives. We shouldn't waste anything."

"Yes, I remember that objectives exercise well," I interjected. "It was on our first day together and seems like a month ago. I do like the idea of seeing failures as raw material, something to work with, not just barriers or downers." I knew I'd never look at failure in the same way—and that was a good thing.

"By analyzing our failures," Chris elaborated, "we discover what doesn't work and what not to do or what not to repeat in the future. But it's important to remember that people are different from machines. Very different! The correct way of dealing with a machine, if there's a problem, is to identify what has gone wrong, so that we can repair or replace it. But I can't emphasize too much that a more positive approach is required with human beings. Machines don't have feelings, whereas people are packed with them."

"We are delicate creatures, aren't we?" I mused.

"That's why the best solution is to analyze our success and achievements. Not only does knowledge of success tell us what actions to try or repeat, but it also has a beneficial effect on our morale and confidence. Think positively!"

"Yes, I know all too well how I feel when I think negatively about myself or receive negative feedback. It's not helpful. I also know that sense of achievement and satisfaction when I'm congratulated for a job well done—as you've done so often. It really reinforces a person's self-esteem."

"Which is exactly what you and all of us need in order to tackle any difficulties with a new or fresh approach," Chris noted. "We need to feel *up*—empowered."

"Why don't we give each other more boosts, instead of the all-too-common thoughtlessness, unkindness, or even meanness?" I asked.

"Good question. You can pin a lot of the blame on that negative programming we've talked about. There's another antidote for that, which I call **Creative Thinking and Living Techniques**. Unlike Sub-Personality Management exercises, these are more in the daily living arena—convenient but less profound, if you will—although they work together for the same end."

"Anything creative has got my vote."

"First, there's what I call **Observation for Awareness**. Most of us don't use our senses to their best advantage—or ours. We need to harness all that sensory power to help us go through life more effectively. We have to realize that sight isn't just the physical act of seeing. It's also a route to perception and understanding. Perceiving requires more awareness and consciousness than mere physical seeing.

"Then there's **Real Listening**, which I referred to just after you arrived. While most people listen, they're usually waiting for the other person to stop, so they can leap in with their own two cents' worth. But the real purpose of conversation should be to form a bridge with another person in order to move the two of you to a new and better place."

"That's novel," I commented, genuinely impressed. "I'm sad to say I'm guilty of the butt-in concept of conversation, as you've probably noticed. I can't wait to add to what the other person is saying, expand on it. I've always believed that was the whole point! I've never thought of talking as a building or bonding exercise. Nice idea."

We were suddenly interrupted by the conductor, who made us both jump when he asked to see our tickets; we'd been so engrossed in our discussion. I dug mine out of my bag then took a slow sip of what was left of my coffee, cold though it was.

It seemed that Chris was trying to raise every element of my being to a new, more efficient level. Truly perceiving. Really listening. How had my senses, my mind, become so numb, neutralized? Were most people in the same state?

"There are other meme-adjusting tools I'd like to share with you," Chris continued, as soon as the conductor had moved on. "The way you go into a conversation is also more significant than most people realize. For example, there's the **First-Five-Words** exercise where you observe the first five words spoken by you and whomever you're speaking with. They reveal a lot about the speakers' mind-sets and are highly underrated clues in the game and management of life.

"As well, we should pay more attention to how sentences are started. The words "**Yes, but . . .**" indicate a more competitive mind-set, whereas "**Yes, and . . .**" are more co-operative. Being aware of this provides an easy guide to change one's automatic, negative programming to something more positive—unless, that is, you really do disagree with what a person is saying and mean 'Yes, but . . . '"

"So much is automatic," I grumbled.

Chris raised his eyebrows in acknowledgement. "Yes, and . . ."

I gave him the grin he deserved.

"You've just reminded me of another common, defeatist, maintain-the-status-quo attitude: the belief that there's no alternative. On the contrary, there are plenty of them—if you stretch your mind. I call it **Compassing Alternatives** because the best alternative is usually in an entirely different direction from what you think it might be."

He picked up a pen and started drawing on the paper he had already placed in front of him. I spied what looked like a slightly askew compass with N, S, W, E roughly added where appropriate.

"Compassing Alternatives is exactly that," he stated, turning the sketch toward me. "You put your problem down on paper and look North, South, West, and East for realistic, viable solutions—or radically dissimilar alternatives. Think creatively, outside the box, as they say. If you want to go to Rome, for example, you don't have to hop on a plane at Heathrow Airport and fly there directly. You could go via Toronto, Tokyo, or even Timbuktu."

He drew three alternative routes on the crooked compass, all of which ended up in Rome. "The key thing to remember is that there's *always* an alternative. Beware of people who say 'Our only option is . . .' or 'We have no choice . . .'"

I burst out laughing. "Those indirect routes may not be the best examples of positive alternatives these days. First, they'd cost a lot of money, and second, think of the carbon footprint caused by all that extra travelling. But I get your point. There are always choices. Most of us don't have that impression, which is tragic. On this theme, do you think we could have travelled to Scotland via Wales? I would have liked to, although we don't have the time."

"Yes, we could have visited my mother in South Wales and dropped in to see my former mother-in-law in the Lake District," Chris responded, his hands flying about in a display of openness and endless possibilities. He could be a lot of fun when he wasn't pressured to save a person's life in a short period of time.

What a devoted friend he'd been, I thought, as I turned to stare out the slightly grime-streaked window. I'd been so fortunate to have had this extraordinary conclusion to my time in the UK.

"We'll just have to enjoy where we are," he concluded. "Ah, look. Can you see York Minster over there? It took 250 years to build, and the time was well spent. It's one of the most magnificent cathedrals in the world. Also, there's a great view of the old city, once you've climbed the 240-plus steps to the top."

Chris informed me that an ancestor of his, who had helped translate the Bible into English, had been the archbishop at York Minister during the turbulent time of Henry VIII.

"How thrilling to have a living, breathing connection to the modern Bible—and the Tudors!" I exclaimed. "Even though they could be a rather treacherous lot."

Those fascinating bits of history added a uniquely personal touch to our sightseeing. Like most of humanity, I remember details much better when there's something concrete to attach them to. Ah, the workings of the brain.

Not long after York, we decided it was time for a picnic. I offered to go to the snack bar for the forks and napkins, which we hadn't managed to acquire in the train station when we "packed" our picnic at the Marks and Spencer food outlet.

While I made my way down the narrow aisles of three or four cars, I checked out the people engaged in one activity or another—reading, playing cards, listening to iPods, sleeping. No one else seemed to be engaged in the fascinating act of Sub-Personality Management!

As often happened in this small crowded country, a surprise awaited me when I reached the snack bar. A woman I had met when I first arrived in London was standing at the end of the queue. "Kathleen!" she cried as I approached. I couldn't remember her name but did remember her face, and we were soon catching up on our respective lives.

"They're throwing you out?" she asked when I told her of my impending, inglorious departure. "But it doesn't make sense. You're not a drain on the economy or anything."

How many times had I heard that? And each time, I had responded with what a long-ago British friend used to describe as "whinge, whine, moan, and complain." No more! Instead, I agreed that it was indeed unfair; however, I was going to make the most of my return. For one thing, it would be good to see my family after too long.

(If only Chris had been able to hear me.)

She informed me that she was off to visit her son, who was attending school in Scotland, and I told her about my castle wedding—well, not mine exactly. We parted after re-exchanging email addresses, such an essential rite in our society. Her name was Ruth, I found out.

A few minutes later, I walked back to our seats, utensils in hand, wondering if the other passengers could tell I was an almost-illegal "alien." Just in case, I tried to look non-threatening. There was too much xenophobia around to take chances, although I was well aware of my privileged status.

Chris and I chatted aimlessly—or relatively aimlessly—as we ate our salads and chewy buns. At one point, he gestured to the west beyond some rolling hills, saying that we weren't far from where he'd been "incarcerated by monks" in a boarding school for ten years—from age eight to eighteen.

His face looked grim.

"How horrible for you," I blurted. "I had no idea you'd had such a difficult childhood."

I hated to think of him locked up in an isolated, probably dreary building with earnest, well-meaning men of the cloth whose freedom was equally limited—but they had more options. On the other hand, that strict upbringing might have given him the analytical tools he was making such good use of in his adult years. I didn't ask about such things though. After noting the bleak expression on his face, I knew he didn't want to go there.

Unlike my past, his wasn't going to be placed under a microscope. Not then.

It didn't take long before Chris had pulled himself out of his momentary funk and we were at it again. Teacher and student moving forward. For him, the present was much more pertinent than the haunting past. *He* wasn't going to wallow in it.

It was a good example.

"I'd like to go back to the whole concept of changing memes and being more emotionally intelligent. As we've discussed, your return home offers an excellent opportunity for some groundbreaking work for you and your family and friends. It's crucial to remember that, as children and young adults, we *have* to be self-centred. We're constantly growing and discovering new features about life and ourselves, concentrating on developing a new human being on the planet.

"As we grow older, most of that work should be complete, although it rarely is. Our adult years are the time to switch the emphasis, go beyond ourselves, and reach out to others, but this requires certain tools, which, again, we aren't always given. With these tools, some I've been sharing with you, we feel empowered, ready to face whatever challenges come our way."

"I know a few challenges that will come my way as soon as I land," I sulked, sliding into my negative comfort zone. Bad attitude. Kill that meme too! There were so many to hack away at. It was like cutting through a thick jungle with a machete. Whack! Whack! Odd image, but it helped.

"Yes," Chris said brightly, "in the first few days, you'll have dozens of chances to use your new skills—because every difficulty provides opportunities. You'll be able to substitute positive habits and attitudes for all those negative memes—which you'll have to keep a constant eye out for."

Had he been reading my mind about killing troublesome memes? Or would my upcoming struggle in Canada be that predictable?

Both, I decided.

"If you deal with difficulties while they're fresh," Chris continued, "you can learn from them as they come along, instead of being overwhelmed by them. That will make it easier to disconnect from your old patterns and reconnect with the new. Sound good?"

"You make it seem so straightforward and, well, natural that I can almost see myself doing it," I said hopefully.

"Almost!" Chris said, throwing his head back in mock shock and surprise. "Never almost. You *will* do it. I know you will. Oh, we're about to pass the area where the Roman Emperor Hadrian built his famous wall to keep out the rebellious northern clans. But before we get to Scotland, I'd like to finish this little lecture of mine."

He looked at me with utmost concentration. "Let's take the failure you turned into an objective about your mother. If I remember correctly, you moved from thinking that you'd failed to help her deal with her grief to the new position that you'll do all you can to help her move beyond it. That's a big change and commitment, so it's best to prepare yourself with some new memes, new software.

"To do this, you have to develop a new framework for looking at the issue—your relationship with your mother. You have to listen and observe carefully, trying to pull out evidence or information you didn't have when you were young, in order to approach the project, for lack of a better word, from a fresh point of view. This will affect your observation of what goes on between your mother and you—and your perception. You can start re-patterning your actions with your mother, along with your reactions."

"That would be heavenly!" I cried a little too loudly. Self-consciously, I dropped my voice to a whisper. "I'm so tired of repeating old, inadequate ways with certain people."

"Again, first and foremost, don't start off with what's wrong with a relationship and why. Move instead to what's right, what's been achieved, and why. Find positive springboards into others' lives. Spend five minutes before any meeting, thinking of their good qualities and how you can be more helpful to him or her.

"After all, by trying to convert *your* negative memes, you can help others convert theirs. At some point, you can even suggest a few of the Sub-Personality Management Techniques we've discussed, such as 3, 2, 1 Reviewing—where they'd look for three things that went right during an encounter, two that went wrong, and one they'd improve."

"Hmmm," I considered. "I'm not sure some of the people I know would be ready for that. It takes a fair amount of self-honesty and, to be frank, determination—even time."

"You're right. In those cases, you can use a less direct route. For example, when someone says something negative and divisive, your role is to turn it around. If someone says he hates weddings, you can remind him of what a nice time you had together at a certain wedding, conjuring up pleasant memories. It's important to listen to another's point of view but also good to pull away from the negative when it seems to be based on habit, rather than real thought.

"Speaking of 3, 2, 1, there's another exercise you can use to review your actions: the **Four-Column Chart**. The critical ingredient to any review is to examine what *actually* happened—not your own, possibly distorted, interpretation. That's what this chart is about. One column itemizes your Observations of what has just occurred, the next your Interpretations: What caused whatever to happen? What was the source or motivation?

"Then there is the 'What Has To Be Done?' column, listing possible follow-up activities, and finally 'How To Do It,' how to carry out whatever has to be done. All of this is designed to help people deal with emotional concerns in a more scientific way, not just blindly reacting and never solving problems."

"I think the problem is that most people believe that all this 'blindly reacting' is the price of being human," I said. "It's what they're used to. They can't even imagine being in control and rational. Emotionally intelligent. Perhaps I'm speaking only for myself, but I doubt it."

"Sadly, you aren't. But people are mistaken. This flailing about isn't necessary. We have conscious minds; we have senses; we need to use them."

Chris suddenly turned his head and looked out the window. "We've just crossed the Scottish border! Let's transform ourselves into dedicated tourists now. I think I've given you enough food for thought for one train ride."

"Yes," I grinned, "you've given me plenty—well-stocked cupboards full!"

It was a bit overwhelming, so many words and thoughts over a few hours, but I appreciated his desire to continue the RTH treatment, even as we travelled to another country. (That was certainly what Scottish nationalists maintained.)

However, would I have the strength and perseverance, once I returned to my *own* country on the other side of the Atlantic, to follow his instructions? I could picture myself phoning Chris in a pinch before or after a difficult rendezvous, begging him to refresh my memory of 3, 2, 1 Reviewing, PARI, or the Four-Column Chart.

The long-distance charges were going to be horrendous!

Before too long, we were running parallel to the dramatic North Sea coastline—looking out at enormous waves this avid swimmer wouldn't dare to take on. Then at last, the old, grey, and beautiful city of Edinburgh. I was twisting my neck in various directions as we passed more or less below Edinburgh Castle, sitting atop a tall, steep rock, which, Chris informed me, had had some structure or other on it since 850 BC.

"Sounds like it could be a little spooky," I joked. "I'm not sure I'd want to bunk *there* overnight." I had also read that the same king, Edward I, who executed William Wallace—or Mel Gibson—had captured the mediaeval version of the castle in 1296, less than a decade before terminating Wallace. And it was there that the ill-fated Mary Queen of Scots had given birth to her son, the future King James VI—known as James I in England. This was followed by more conflict and conquest—even a "Lang" or Long Siege.

The present castle, towering above us, was constructed in the 1500s and had been a tourist attraction since 1818. That year, the prolific novelist and poet Sir Walter Scott (*Ivanhoe*, *The Lady of the Lake*) helped to break into a dusty, cobwebbed-filled (I would imagine) room where the so-called "Honours" of Scotland—the

Crown, Sword, and Sceptre—had been stored since the unification of England and Scotland more than a century earlier.

Some had doubted they were still there, but, after Scott uncovered them, the public was welcomed to come and see for themselves.

Once we had switched trains in the atmospheric Edinburgh Waverley train station, we crossed over the Firth of Forth and passed close to St. Andrews, the legendary home of golf. Chris told me proudly that the town was also known for its university where his soon-to-be-wed son, Joel, met his bride-to-be.

(More recently, where a certain future king, William, met his bride, Kate.)

Then it was over the River Tay and the city of Dundee, a name that made me want to perform a short jig. Maybe later. Finally, as the light was fading, we arrived at Stonehaven, once an Iron Age (which came after the Bronze Age a few thousand years ago BC) fishing village.

Pulling our suitcases behind us, we made our way to the nearby bed and breakfast where Chris had reserved two small rooms in a sturdy, old house. After a lively, wee chat with the charming couple running the place, we put our bags in our respective rooms, freshened up, and set out to wander through the town to the seaside.

There, we found a friendly restaurant with an impressive display of whisky above the bar—which we eagerly sampled as the regular patrons looked on, laughing, joking, and having a gay old time. With their evocative taste of peat, our drams went down very well after the long journey.

We were truly in deep Scotland!

For dinner, we ate a local dish called Cullen (after a Scottish town) Skink (don't ask—alright, skink has something to do with a shin of beef, although I don't think there was any), not far from a huge fireplace.

The ambiance couldn't have been homier and the Cullen Skink with its generous chunks of smoked haddock—a.k.a. Finnan (named after another Scottish community) Haddie (short for haddock) with potatoes, onions, and lots of cream—was nothing less than ambrosia. Did I dare ask for the recipe?

Or google it.

After our meal, we were determined to do our best to soak up the atmosphere, so we ordered more scotch, pulled our chairs in front of the fire, since we were the only customers left, and talked until past midnight.

It was then that Chris provided me with a tad more of his professional and non-professional background. He elaborated on his work, years ago, with the international personal development company, which he'd helped to expand around the globe. This had called for a lot of travel and had probably led to the end of his first marriage. Not long after his divorce, he'd left the organization, vowing to use his knowledge on a smaller, more intimate level—one that didn't require a suitcase.

Sipping my single malt, I realized that I was one of the lucky beneficiaries of that decision, but was again thankful I hadn't come to Chris specifically for relationship advice—although, needless to say, that had entered into our therapeutic work together.

On the other hand, I was sure his own difficult path added to his supply of teaching tools, which was always an asset. It's tough to confide in someone who hasn't a clue what you're talking about, can't identify with your trials and tribulations.

As if reading my mind—nothing new—my mentor noted that the collapse of *both* his marriages had shown him that, no matter how much you think you know, you must always keep learning—and applying what you learn.

A valid conclusion.

CHAPTER THIRTEEN

It Is the Journey

*It is good to have an end to journey toward; but
it is the journey that matters, in the end.*
—Ursula K. Le Guin

We rose early enough the next sunny but chilly morning to have plenty of time to feast on our heavy Scottish breakfast, chat at length with our hosts, and walk to the town square—where we met Ben, Chris's bright and very appealing younger son from his second marriage.

As the three of us strolled toward the sea, I heard my mobile phone ringing and excused myself from the others. It was Julian. He wanted to make sure my trip had gone well. I was predictably thrilled to hear from him, but also resented his intrusion into my attempt to get on with my life—as he had insisted so often he wanted me to do.

"Where are you?" he asked.

"I'm walking along the sea surrounded by gulls and fishing boats. It's lovely. I'm so happy to be here." Was that convincing?

"Well, I just wanted to make sure you were all right. I do miss you, you know."

"That's nice." Don't weaken! "Thanks so much for calling. I'm fine and I'll see you on Monday. Only two days to go."

We said our goodbyes, and I hung up with a sigh of relief. In spite of my efforts to stay and sound strong, our awkward chat had thrown me off balance. Pulled the rug out from under . . . Why couldn't I put that vulnerable state of mind behind me? What would it take to strengthen my . . . my strength?

When I apologized for the interruption, Chris, obviously aware of what had just happened, discreetly held up three fingers, then two, then one. Ah, I translated silently, 3, 2, 1 Reviewing! Here? Now? I quickly summed up the conversation, telling myself that the Three Things That Went Right were that I was upbeat, strong, and, I hoped, convincing. The Two Things That Went Wrong were that I could almost hear my heart pounding and was quite miserable.

The Thing I Would Change was to be a lot more in control of my feelings.

While I was going through this mental exercise as swiftly as possible, Chris suggested we explore one of Stonehaven's major attractions, Dunnottar Castle, perched precariously on a rocky outcrop over the rough waters of the North Sea.

Why not? I enthused. I'm ready for another challenge!

As we started hiking to the haunting ruin, Chris gave me a wink and, with great gusto, began a small history lecture. Was he once again trying to put my own problems into perspective? Easy to do in those surroundings.

In 1296, Chris told us, the same English king, Edward I, who attacked Edinburgh while on a rampage across Scotland, also took over Dunnottar Castle. But his arch-nemesis William Wallace (Mel) recaptured it and, according to legend, burned down the nearby church—with the entire English garrison inside. (That will often get you executed.)

A few centuries later, in 1650, Oliver Cromwell sacked the castle in search of the Scottish Crown Jewels, but they had been smuggled away by some local women, who took them by boat to a village down the coast. The jewels weren't discovered for nine years. Let's hope those daring women weren't found out!

I learned later that the controversial Mel Gibson did appear to like those northern climes. In 1990, he starred in the movie *Hamlet*, which was partly filmed at Dunnottar Castle. I could picture him prowling around the cold stone walls in unfettered Shakespearian angst.

To be or not to be . . . in Denmark, Scotland, or Hollywood.

In some ways, I felt that I too was starring in a fascinating movie, packed with change and suspense, although I wasn't yearning to live the life of Shakespeare's ill-fated Ophelia. I certainly wasn't about to get myself to a nunnery or go mad and drown in a brook—even though Millais had made it all look so pretty.

My relationship with Julian was theatrical enough for this modern girl; I wanted a less dramatic and traumatic ending!

After our Dunnottar tour, during which Ben and I scampered around the ancient stones like a couple of kids, the three of us were picked up by Chris's older, about-to-be-hitched son and whisked across the peaceful countryside to Drumtochty Castle, near the village of Auchenblae.

It was an odd group in the car—Chris, his two sons, and me—but cheery and casual. I got the impression the young men knew something about my being RTHed, asking me about Wimbledon and their father's cooking, and suspected they weren't entirely new to meeting Chris's various friends and acquaintances.

When we arrived at *our* castle, I was glad to see that it wasn't as moody or even as historic as Dunnottar—or Edinburgh. To my untrained eye, each of these mighty structures seemed to have its own personality and, fortunately, Drumtochy's wasn't at all menacing or mediaeval.

Instead, it was a welcoming, Victorian castle with all the required accoutrements: a 350-acre estate, turrets, parapets, an entrance hall with a soaring cathedral ceiling—or Gothic vault, I was told—antlers on the walls, antiques and armour, blazing fires. No wonder its advertising slogan was "Live life like a Laird."

Or Lady—as I planned to do for the rest of the day and night.

There was just one complication. On our arrival, Joel announced that he had reserved the biggest bedroom in the place for us. Bedroom? Singular? I tried not to react visibly, keeping a stiff grin on my face. So far, Chris and I had managed to maintain a safe distance from each other as mentor and student or life coach and coachee, but now we would be spending the night in the same room.

Same bed!

Being the last-minute guest, I said nothing as we followed Joel along the central hall, out the side door, and around to the back of the huge building where an entire living area, including a kitchen, had been added. We then climbed to the top floor via thickly carpeted stairs, and I waited with bated breath as Joel opened the door.

"This is one of the most impressive rooms in the castle," the young man informed us proudly, as he stepped aside to let us enter.

Neither Chris nor I made a peep in protest. Instead, we sincerely praised the enormous, bright red room, dominated by one ornate, regal-sized bed. There were flowers and a welcome card from the about-to-be-married couple on an equally ornate mahogany dressing table. (Even in that difficult moment, I remembered how much I loved dressing tables, sitting down to brush my hair, spreading out my makeup in front of the mirror, pretending to be in some 1940s movie.)

"It's a great room," I heard Chris say to his son, who was obviously eager to attend to other pre-wedding details.

"Yes," I agreed, possibly too enthusiastically. And soon we were alone.

Chris turned to me. "I'm so sorry. I thought I'd made it clear that we wanted two rooms, but perhaps I was too subtle. It was all a bit rushed. I'm more than willing to make other arrangements now though. I don't want this to lessen our counselling relationship—or our friendship."

"Well, I'm fine with it, if you are," I said brightly. "We're equals, not doctor and patient, even though we've joked about that a few times. I don't feel taken advantage of. Besides, five people could sleep in this bed and they wouldn't even have to introduce themselves; they'd be so far apart. Oh, one more thing. I trust you! Do you trust me?" I raised my eyebrows slightly.

Then I dropped them quickly, fearing such a gesture could be misleadingly provocative. Why were there so many social inhibitions and potential sexual pitfalls, even with two mature people trying so hard to be honest with each other?

"I most certainly do trust you. More than you know," Chris said rather mysteriously.

We each found a spot for our suitcases and busied ourselves unpacking and hanging up crucial items of clothing in our cupboards. Although it wasn't an absolute necessity, I wondered where they might store a steam iron in this enormous place. Or would that be too un-Victorian?

Since there were a few hours before the late-afternoon wedding ceremony and we didn't appear to be needed, Chris and I decided to take a tour of the castle and gardens before dressing for the big event. We put on our coats and boots and were soon prowling around indoors, finding such features as a games room (a must for knights on dull evenings, we agreed), a library, a bar, and a hot tub. (Wouldn't that rust the knights' armour? I asked.)

Outside, we walked to one edge of the yard and gazed down on a small river with a sweet, tantalizing bridge arching to a tiny island. Soon, we were following the path leading to this little scene, crossing the bridge cautiously, and standing on the water-encircled piece of land. It was all quite dreamlike as the snow began to fall.

"Thank you for inviting me to this paradise," I sighed. "You've been so good to me."

"I think you know that I've enjoyed every minute of our time so far," Chris said solemnly. "I could wring the necks of the UK authorities for bringing it all to an end."

"I wouldn't stop you!" I replied, and we both fell silent as we looked across to the other side of the river and the whitening fields.

After our tour, which also included Chris's bumping into former in-laws and introducing me as his friend, we went back to our room to change for the wedding. Fortunately, Chris decided to shave and retreated to the enormous bathroom next to us for quite a while. When he returned, I was reading a book on a red velvet Sarah Bernhardt–style chaise longue, dressed and ready to go.

Chris quickly donned his tuxedo, which had been rented by Joel and was hanging neatly pressed in the cupboard; we put on our winter gear and wended our way to the small chapel at the bottom of the hill. As we walked along the snow-covered road, we noticed that there weren't many others who had chosen to go by foot, in spite of the short distance. Someone suggested that this was probably because most of the women had worn high-heeled shoes and needed to be driven.

I looked down at my boots. They weren't exactly castle garb—or wedding, for that matter. They were more like something you would wear, well, walking in the snow. But there you go. I promised myself I'd make more effort in the elegance department when I was no longer living out of a suitcase.

The chapel was beautifully decorated with small candles flickering everywhere and the music of Vivaldi, played by a quintet in one corner, filling the air. A beaming Ben led Chris and me to the front. He indicated that I should sit in the third row amongst the groom's relatives—total strangers who smiled sweetly—and led Chris to the front pew to sit beside his first wife, the mother of the groom.

Shortly after he sat down and they had begun talking, she turned around to locate me, and we nodded. It was all very, very civilized, although my life coach's second wife, Ben's mother, had apparently sent her regrets.

The ceremony was simple, sincere, and quite chilly—at least for the bride, Harriet, who wore a gorgeous strapless gown. It was easy to imagine the discomfort of weddings in the past before the invention of the necessary space heaters, which kept those of us wrapped in coats reasonably warm. After the rings had been exchanged and the music had swelled to a final crescendo, we poured out into the crisp, outdoor air, and some brave souls, including Chris and me, stomped our way back up the hill to our castle.

The rest of the afternoon and evening were also magical: cocktails followed by a luscious meal of pheasant in the enormous reception area and dancing wildly with Chris—who looked natural and suave in his tuxedo—and others to a Scottish Ceilidh band. Once in a while throughout the marvellous celebration, I took a needed break in front of the roaring fire, chatting with numerous friendly and welcoming fellow guests—probably wondering who the heck I was.

Finally, we all walked out in front of the castle under the starry sky, lit small fires inside Japanese paper lanterns, and carefully released them to rise above the trees. It was like letting all our hopes for the glowing newlyweds—and ourselves—leave the confines of the earth and float wherever they needed to go to become reality. I closed my eyes after my lantern had vanished into the distant black and wished for a happy, directed, productive future—with Julian.

Tired, Chris and I made our way up the plush stairs well after midnight. We each took turns in the spacious loo, while the other hurriedly prepared for bed. Then we pulled down the thick, brocaded bedspread and climbed in.

"I hope you don't feel too uncomfortable with all this," I heard Chris say softly in the dark. Half asleep after quantities of champagne and too many Highland jigs, I reached over and held his big warm hand. I didn't have the emotional or physical energy to say or do anything more complicated.

Sunday morning in the castle was jolly. We were treated to an endless supply of eggs, fruit, cheeses, breads, juices, and cups of coffee laid out on a long table in a sunny room with tall, paned windows overlooking the river. There was a real feeling of camaraderie after the touching nuptials we had witnessed.

Even my recent confusion and growing cynicism about love was peeled back to expose a true sentimental side. That old line that marriage was the triumph of hope over experience seemed dusty and sad. Joining together two people who love each other in some recognized way was a blessed thing to do, I convinced myself.

Blessed, but was it possible for this wanderer?

After breakfast, Chris and I joined another couple for a more ambitious walking tour of the estate. It was my last opportunity to appreciate the heart-tugging rural beauty of this part of the world, and I tried to savour every precious step.

We were then chauffeured to the station, where we settled into the train for the long journey to London. Of course, during this trip we would be seeing everything from a north to south perspective, and it was fascinating how much difference that usually made to the general effect.

Now, I told myself as I rested my head contentedly against the back of my seat, it was relaxation and appreciation time after our wonderful, whirlwind weekend.

Chris had other ideas!

"Kathleen, I've certainly enjoyed having you with me on this trip, but it's been a bit of a test, you know. I wanted your company, but I also wanted to see you in a difficult, more sociable environment—and you passed with ease. Everyone loved you."

"I felt completely comfortable, especially because I didn't realize it was an examination!"

Chris shrugged. "I don't want to be too harsh at this point, but from the beginning, you've reminded me of that analogy of a solid-looking house resting on a weak foundation. The house is very liveable, indeed; the foundation definitely requires reinforcing. I do hope you won't forget what you've learned over the past two weeks."

"It would help if you could be around a lot longer with your hammer and nails," I teased. "Or maybe a truckload of cement!

Seriously, I've realized too much about myself to turn back now. I promise."

Imagine how I felt when Chris eyed me inquisitively from across the table and asked if I wanted to do two last exercises before returning to Canada.

I cowered at the thought—not of doing the exercises but of leaving the country. It would be good to see my loved ones. My daughter. I knew that. However, I was realizing more and more that I fit into *this* world so much better. I always had—ever since my first school trip to Europe when I was sixteen.

During that unforgettable vacation, the sights, sounds, and flavours of the new-for-me Old World had made my senses sit up and take notice. My under-developed taste buds were particularly tantalized. The first time some classmates and I conspired to buy cheese, bread, and white wine in a German town and smuggle them past our chaperones into our hotel room, I was hooked. I'd never known such richness. No more soft drinks and potato chips for this teenager.

And that was *before* we reached Paris!

Decades later, there I was, being enticed by Europe yet again, and preparing to depart, yet again. Wistfully, I told Chris I would love to wrap up our RTH efforts with something stimulating—and he certainly took me at my word. He asked me to do nothing less than write my own **Eleven-Word Epitaph**.

"Sum up your Ideal Life in as succinct a way as possible," he said. "I know it won't be easy, but we have plenty of time. No rush." He put his head back against his seat and glanced out the window.

Like so many exercises before, I was faced with the task of looking inward. Now I had to look inward and forward at the same time. As if that weren't difficult enough, how was I going to sum up my life in eleven measly words? After what seemed like ages—I think we had crossed the English border—I managed, with regular glances out the window, to put together the following: "She loved, created, and helped change the world for the better."

Count them. Eleven!

I sat quietly looking at my words until I could detect some movement from Chris, who seemed to have fallen asleep. When his eyes opened, I handed him my Epitaph (bizarre though it felt). He read it quietly and then smiled.

"Now would you mind expanding this to a full-blown **Obituary**? Just a few paragraphs like the ones you find in most daily papers. Not an autobiography. How would you like your Obit to read in decades to come—when that sad occasion arises? I'm interested, and I'm sure you are too."

Obituary? Yes, the summation of my life lived in so many words. How I would like to be remembered by one and all. What mark I would like to make—or have made. What a thought! It certainly transformed the act of carving out an existence, a personal story, into quite a responsibility—even if the whole purpose was simply to have a few decent lines in the local paper. An item people would read over their tea and toast in the morning.

"Some people find it constructive to look forward by looking back, if that makes any sense," Chris explained. "Writing your Obituary will give you the means to seriously identify what you want your life to be like over the next several years. You've already defined your Ideal Life for me in the abstract. This gives your thoughts more substance. It will give you a road map of sorts."

"I could use a road map," I said. "You've given me several of what you might call road signs, which have been very helpful. And you're right. I need to have some sense of how they all fit together—where they are leading." I halted. "But an Obituary? It sounds so morbid."

Chris laughed his hearty laugh. "I know. Our society doesn't like to deal with death, the fate-that-dares-not-speak-its-name, but it *is* a reality. A rather definite one. It's non-negotiable. So I think it's necessary to acknowledge and work with it. What I'm asking is that you put yourself at the end of your life and envision what you would truly like to be the sum total of all your days and nights. Your actions and efforts. This is a good way to focus your thoughts and wishes."

Before long, I took the pad of paper on the table in front of me and wrote the words "My Obituary" in fairly large letters. I then rested my head and stared at the rolling fields passing by. What would I like to be able to look back on when the time came to look back one last time? Chris was spot on, as usual. This exercise really did make me identify my priorities.

Eventually, with a fair amount of thinking and rethinking, writing and rewriting, this is what I produced for Chris to read:

My Obituary

Kathleen O'Hara died of natural causes last night after a long and rich life. Her family and friends were with her—some of them via the Internet—as she closed her eyes for the last time. Her final words, "I have loved all of you and life itself. I have no regrets," summed up her ninety years of productive, satisfying activities.

Kathleen got off to a rough start with the early death of her father and her mother's difficulties raising a large family alone. For many years, Kathleen, the eldest, was quite lost and even confused. She wasn't able to establish a life that satisfied her and expressed her bountiful energy and concerns for the world.

However, this changed after she spent an unexpected six months in London, UK. For various reasons—in particular, precious time spent with her life coach and friend, Chris C.—this period allowed her thoughts and desires to jell as they had never done before. After making a serious effort to define and know herself as well as is humanly possible, she started out on a vital path that didn't cease until her death.

In recent decades, she has worked tirelessly writing books about self-knowledge and humanity's role on this planet. She has volunteered and worked for several progressive organizations, focussing on climate change and bringing peace to the world. She has been a major voice on various panels at international conferences, as well as radio and television. Her opinions were highly valued as she brought together the need for inner development and real solutions to external problems plaguing the globe.

Kathleen's life also changed when she met and married Julian B. These two human beings realized at first sight that they were perfect for each other. Julian loved Kathleen's energy, enthusiasm, sociability, and commitment. And Kathleen loved Julian's sense of humour and laugh, his kind and nurturing personality, his appreciation for the arts, and his humane and caring politics. Together, they broadened each other's lives in a healthy and joyous partnership.

Although Kathleen had family in Canada, she and Julian settled themselves in Julian's home in Highgate, which they transformed into a warm and welcoming base. Over the years, they spent many months at a time visiting friends and relatives, or travelling—with as small a carbon footprint as possible. They both loved photographing, drawing, and painting the various places of interest they discovered together. Many observers, known and unknown, admired their adoration for and dedication to each other, and their sense of fun. Julian died a few months before Kathleen, so she had to live without him for only a short while.

Kathleen was particularly proud of her beloved daughter, Wren. Wren's career as a professor of political economy, after she attained her PhD, often provided the academic backup for Kathleen's own work. Mother and daughter were partners in their efforts to transform society. This gave Kathleen more joy than her own singular accomplishments. Their closeness was her greatest source of fulfillment.

Living and working with those she cared for were the most important aspects of life for Kathleen. She was also close to her four brothers and sisters, their children and grandchildren, many of whom were by her side when she died. They all respected her kindness, generosity, and wisdom, and knew she was happy and content until the end.<

After putting the paper down on the table in front of him, Chris said nothing for the longest time. I had seen tears welling up in his eyes as he read, and tried to guess what was going through his head. I thought of how often Julian had wept over the apparent impossibility of "us" and wondered if this was a common male reaction in the UK. If so, I liked it. It was both sincere and honest. A quivering upper lip was much better than a stiff one.

"I'm moved," he said at last. "Truly moved. This shows me that we've accomplished a lot together. You get it! You haven't played mind games or compromised. Your goals are specific and realistic. They're you."

He looked down at the page. It wasn't like him to be at a loss for words.

I said nothing.

"So many people are afraid to put themselves out there, if you know what I mean. They don't want to make themselves vulnerable, or they're afraid of others' reactions. But you've really hit it. You've been precise and honest. You *do* know what you want—and it's something worth aiming and fighting for. After all, as someone once said, if you are going to play the game, it might as well be the right one."

"Yes," I said, "you've made me realize that. You've made me realize many things."

"I've enjoyed every second of it. However, I'm not going to let you off the hook or onto the plane without one last piece of advice."

He leaned across the table between us, took hold of my hands, and looked me straight in the eye. "Now you must act!"

But there was a gleam in those gentle eyes that made me certain we would be friends forever, no matter how My Obit eventually read. Our time together at the Railway Tracks Hotel and elsewhere had been a little like our train trip. We had travelled together far, fast, and well.

We had seen and learned so much, so very much.

EPILOGUE

The next day, Julian picked me up in the parking area outside Chris's townhouse. I wouldn't let him come to the door.

I had thanked and said goodbye to my coach/host/mentor/friend in his living room where so many memorable moments had occurred over such a short time. For some reason, which I couldn't quite explain, I didn't want the two men—the yin and the yang—to meet.

Perhaps I preferred to keep the more or less negative and confusing aspect of my life—Julian—away from the positive and focussed part—Chris. I didn't want the former to contaminate the latter or render it less effective. And I knew I wasn't strong enough yet to deal with any possible conflict between both realms.

My plane didn't leave until early evening, but Julian had suggested picking me up before noon to give us more time together. The irony of this after his not wanting to see me for a week was not lost on me, but I decided to rise above such concerns. I had grovelled too much already and was now turning a corner.

I wanted to leave the country with at least some dignity intact.

After throwing my smaller suitcase in the boot of his car beside the larger one he had been storing, Julian proposed that we drive to Windsor for lunch. It was on the way to Heathrow Airport. Needless to say, as we zipped along the roadway, talking and laughing in our usual fashion, I had an impending sense of doom—knowing that all this joy and companionship was coming to an end.

In the pretty town of Windsor, we prowled around its picture-perfect river dotted with graceful swans, then walked along the High Street, happily examining store window displays, to historic Eton College. Finally, we chose an attractive riverside restaurant, looking directly across at Windsor Castle.

From our table, we could see that the castle's flag was flying at full mast, indicating that the Queen was in residence, which was nice to know. Maybe she too was about to sit down to a meal, I joked, and was staring at us!

Should we wave?

Julian laughed, but became serious before handing me a letter he wanted me to read on the plane—and a small box that I could open then and there.

When I did, I was taken aback. There was a small, round, silver medallion with St. Christopher, the patron saint of travellers, carved into the metal. Near the bottom, not far from the saint's foot, an uncut ruby, like a pink pearl, had been exquisitely embedded by Julian's local jeweller. On the other side, an inscription read, "To take care of my sweet K."

Instantly, my heart began to pound; my stomach felt sick. In fact, I was so overcome I had to leave the table and head downstairs to the loo, where I burst into miserable tears. Leila had been right. My obstinate lover's gestures could be both beautiful and cruel.

I didn't return until I'd pulled myself together and dug into my reservoir of Chris's lessons and advice. Now was the time to show Julian, and myself, that I had emerged from the RTH a different kind of person—not completely revolutionized, but changed.

"This is a thoughtful farewell gift, Julian. I will cherish it forever," I said calmly, as I sat back down opposite him. "You've been very good to me over the past several months, and I will never forget it."

Julian looked pale. This wasn't easy for him either. I continued speaking, wanting to make sure I delivered the message I had concocted in the loo.

"I plan to be quite productive when I am in Canada. In fact, I've put together a mental to-do list and can't wait to get started. But I do hope we can stay in touch while I'm remodelling my life."

Julian's eyes were gleaming with tears. He looked at me with such love and devotion I almost threw away all that determination and converted to woe-is-me mode. But Chris's words and faith haunted me and kept me going. I didn't back down.

Instead, I reached for a crusty, freshly baked bun and took a rather large bite.

So there!

Our actual parting was even more difficult. Once I had checked my larger bag, Julian and I sat on a couch in the airport bar and talked, glancing at the clock above our heads every once in a while. The seconds were ticking away, and there was no way to stop them. In spite of this, I maintained my cool. I was still basking in the glow of my newly discovered strength and had a sense of power—over myself—I hadn't known before.

Nevertheless, as Julian accompanied me slowly to the security gate, each step seemed more foreboding than the last—a tiny bit like being led to the gallows. That feeling of being close to the end of something that has been emotionally all-consuming is not fun. Finally, we hugged, cried, promised to get together soon, and parted.

I walked through security with my head held as high as it would go.

When I landed back home, I suffered from a deep sadness caused by the loss of someone and some things valued in my life. Julian's letter had given me no grounds for real hope; I felt flattened, diminished. However, I tried to carry on as best I could. What else can a person do?

Grieving is a process that can't be rushed.

During the first months, Julian called a few times—sometimes sounding quite fragile. He wrote friendly emails, saying he missed me, but that was all. He made no plans to visit; he sent no invitations. I tried to take the jolly high road, keeping him informed of my busy life, my family, my friends.

As always, our deep attachment couldn't be ignored or thrown away completely by either of us. On the other hand, as I began to build my present existence the way I wanted it to be, I had less time or desire to pine over a man who couldn't or wouldn't love me enough. Slowly, we began to write less frequently, simply reporting our news in a genial sort of way. The thrill—and the pain—was gone.

My Obituary already needed reworking!

During this transition period, I continued to rely on the wisdom and experience of others, reading about spirituality, mindfulness, and positive thinking. Chris had laid the groundwork for powerful self-awareness and forward movement, and I wasn't going to let it dissolve due to forgetfulness or lack of use.

It is much, much too easy to slip into past patterns—and problems. I'm sure we all know that.

Before we parted, my life coach had suggested I think of **Five Skills, Strengths, and Qualities** of every "difficult" person I might encounter, which I began to do as soon as I got settled on the plane. No time to waste! As I'd learned at the Railway Tracks Hotel, we generally aren't taught the techniques to prepare ourselves emotionally and psychologically for most of the challenges thrown our way, but they can be acquired—with effort.

In fact, one of my sisters commented on my newfound patience and diplomacy after she had witnessed my cool handling of a couple of events that, she admitted, would have thrown her into despair for days. Yes, now that I had my eye on the much larger, more positive ball, I was able to RTH my way through minor skirmishes—although it continued to be a struggle.

Speaking of balls, I took up tennis. My instinct told me that a sport requiring precision and concentration would be the perfect supplement to my attempts to make my conscious mind sharper and more effective. (I also cut down on my alcohol intake!)

However, tennis wasn't just good for my mind. It had an uplifting influence on my self-image—biking to the club with a racquet in my basket, dashing around the courts surrounded by neatly dressed athletes, developing another skill to add to my list.

Chris had shown me how important self-image is—the basis of everything, actually—and had uncovered the fact that mine wasn't exactly top-of-the-line. I had always had an image of myself as thin and fit, so no stretch there, but I had also seen myself as a victim, a loser.

Thanks to the RTH, I've been reversing that image with every tennis game, set, and match—and enjoying the consequences. Love-Me! I am becoming an actor, not a victim; a winner, not a loser. Someone who has defined her purposes in life and is determined to follow them.

I took up gardening, working with the earth, creating, and being immersed in nature. For this reason, I joined the organizing committee—with nuns, farmers, and others—of the determined Save Our Prison Farms campaign. The Conservative Canadian government had announced it was cutting an internationally acclaimed rehabilitation programme at six prisons across the country where inmates produced their own food and gained self-respect, as well as acquiring useful work skills. Knowing what I now knew, I couldn't stand by and watch people being deprived of an opportunity to learn and move forward.

And I joined the Transition Town movement, which aims to help communities around the world move from the increasingly unrealistic, destructive, and globalized oil-based economy to a more sustainable, community-based way of living.

Generally, I've been building on my need to be engaged in meaningful activity, as well as my ability to make a difference—and this has given me a priceless sense of fulfillment. As well, putting my own life into perspective has made it easier to deepen my connections with others. For one thing, my mother and I now have regular lunches with long, easy-going conversations, opening new doors.

My new accomplishments, activism, and attitude are all thanks to the mental turnaround that Chris led me toward, although I am still prone to relapses of insecurity and uncertainty. There have been nights when I've suffered from what I call "frustration dreams," during which I can't find someone, can't get somewhere, can't, can't, can't.

They're becoming rarer.

Rome certainly wasn't built in a day—or a year.

The real proof of my transformation is in your hands! In spite of the uphill climb, I wrote this book. Just hours after I got off the plane and recovered from jet lag, I picked up my computer and started typing—on living-room couches, verandas, park benches, in bed. I didn't stop for several months. What gave me the impetus was the fact that I finally knew it was my *right* to write.

As each chapter was completed, I emailed it to Chris, my advisor in Wimbledon. We weren't in the same place as collaborators, but we were working together virtually—and well. He kept me going with his positive and enthusiastic, but honest and helpful feedback. This didn't come as any surprise!

Others, like dear Ted, also supported me. He even claimed to be my "biggest admirer." Some people simply care.

Remember how I wanted to change the world and people's lives with my writing? Well, I've realized that the only way that can happen is if enough people take the RTH challenge, start to resist all those negative, I'm-not-that-important memes, and begin to change themselves and their societies.

This book may not be revolutionary, as in marching through the streets and overthrowing unpopular governments, but my hope is that it can start a slow, steady wave of positive movement—with people realizing who they are and what they can do.

One after another after another.

So finally, it's over to you. I invite you to follow the path I have mapped out with Chris's help. It's not well-worn, but the view along the way is interesting, exciting, and beautiful. Exhilarating!

Of course, with this particular path there is no tangible end, no clear finish. That's because none of us can ever complete our self-learning, self-enhancement journey—and then sit back and rest on our well-earned laurels. Would we want to? How dull is that?

Right now, all I ask is that when you close this book you begin to take the first steps to change, the way I have. As Chris said to me, "Now you must act!"

RTH GLOSSARY OF TERMS

Life Coach (Prologue/Chapter Four): A life coach works with you to help you grow, develop, and make a success of your life. He or she is like a professionally trained friend—knowledgeable, reliable, there when needed, and ready to give direction and advice when asked.

Co-Counselling (Prologue): Unlike traditional therapist/patient counselling, co-counselling involves teaming up with others to share problems and solutions. It should be mutual and equal and can even be done via the Internet—e-co-counselling.

Direction-Finding Techniques (Chapter One): These exercises and methods, often guided by a life coach, involve delving into yourself through a variety of routes in order to really know who you are, what you think, and where you should be heading. They help you discover the real you.

Behavioural-Change Coaching (Chapter Four): Like life coaching, this practice helps people change their programmed, unconscious behaviour. It has come a long way over the past twenty years. Today's approaches are based on developments in a variety of disciplines, including sports, management education, consciousness studies, behavioural sciences, and cognitive research.

Cognition (Chapter Four): The mental processes that allow you to acquire and use knowledge.

Four Personal Development Strands (Chapter Four): There are four key RTH development areas: Mental, Spiritual, Emotional, and Physical. For each, activities exist to help in the related development process.

Obstinacity Principle (Chapter Five): Weaknesses are really strengths that have been mistimed or misapplied. What is perceived to be "obstinacy" in one circumstance will be seen as "tenacity" in another.

Meme (Chapter Seven): The name given by the British scientist Richard Dawkins to the individual units that transmit a particular behaviour from person to person or group to group—and there are plenty. Memes are the systems, procedures, laws, rules, habits, programmes, routines, and conventions that govern the way we live our lives.

Memetics (Chapter Seven): The study of memes. Just as genetics is the study of genes and the transmission of physical characteristics to future generations, so memetics is the study of memes and the transmission of behaviours within or between cultures. With memetics, we can isolate the various factors in a society that cause people to behave in predictable ways.

Memetic Engineering (Chapter Seven): The process whereby we can isolate negative memes that cause unwanted behaviour in ourselves and others and replace them with new, positive memes that result in desirable behaviour. Memetic engineering is all about controlling our unconscious minds. By changing our memes, we can change our unconscious reactions and responses.

Sub-Personality Management (Chapter Nine): Paying close attention to what we might consider habits or key parts of our personality. These can be adjusted or overruled with conscious effort.

Creative Thinking and Living (Chapter Twelve): This involves finding new and better ways to think about your own life and actions—and acting on them.

APPENDIX A

RTH Exercises/Techniques

DIRECTION-FINDING TECHNIQUES

Top Twenty Accomplishments (Chapter One): List your greatest achievements from childhood to the present. Too many of us forget what we have really and truly accomplished in a variety of areas.

Top Ten Failures (Chapter One): No more than ten! The point is to identify failures in order to transform them into Positive Objectives for the future.

Top Ten Values and Standards (Chapter Four/Nine): This exercise comes under the Spiritual Development strand. List the criteria by which you measure yourself, your attitudes, and your actions as a parent, son, daughter, partner, colleague, neighbour, and so on. What grounds your soul and inspires your spirit. What you stand for!

Top Twenty Skills, Strengths, and Qualities (SSQs) (Chapter Five): List your top twenty SSQs. These too are generally undefined and under-appreciated as we make our way through life. Without identifying them, we can't build on them.

Ten Weaknesses (Chapter Five): Again, no more than ten! The goal here is simply to achieve a balance with your SSQs and move to the exercise below.

Weaknesses into Strengths (Chapter Five): Weaknesses are only strengths mistimed or misapplied. After listing your weaknesses, try to identify the underlying strengths. For example, if you identified one of your weaknesses as "always finding fault," this could indicate that you are strong in negative analysis. If you focus this ability on people, it can be destructive, but if you aim it at harmful systems, traditions, or rules, it could be useful and positive.

Five Occasions When You Felt Really Good About Your Actions, Behaviour, or Role (Chapter Six): This list is again about finding positives in your life. Once written, it should be used to establish the reasons why you felt really good. These reasons can then be used to identify more SSQs and interests—in order to determine future action.

Five Occasions When You Felt Really Bad About Your Actions, Behaviour, or Role (Chapter Six): This list is another route to knowing yourself. It should be used to discover the reasons why you felt bad. They can then be used to identify failures, which can usually be turned into Positive Objectives. Your negatives should never go unused!

Characteristics of an Ideal Human Being (Chapter Eight): Rate yourself as accurately as you can in relation to a variety of human characteristics. See list below in Appendix B.

Five Main Positive Characteristics from Others' Point of View (Chapter Nine): Write down the Five Main Characteristics your family, friends, colleagues, and others might value in you. This will again help you identify your SSQs—and your future.

Who You Are (Chapter Ten): Pretend you are speaking to a stranger on a train and want to sum up exactly who you are in a short, clear paragraph or two. Be as clear, precise, and honest as you can be. It should be a powerful summary.

Your Ideal Life (Chapter Ten): What is your life wish list? What do you want it to be like right now and into the future? It really helps to write it down. Be as clear and honest as you can be, basing it on what you've learned from the previous exercises.

What Is in Your Behaviour/Attitude That Prevents You from Achieving Your Goals/Stretching Yourself? (Chapter Ten): What is stopping you from making progress toward your goals or the Ideal Life you've outlined? What are the characteristics within you that repeatedly get in the way and prevent you from making progress? Identifying the weaknesses that repeatedly hold us up is half the battle. Once we know what they are, we can ask for help from our life coach, counsellor, co-counsellor, even family and friends to overcome them.

Necessary Developments Within Yourself That Would Contribute to Your Becoming an Ideal Human Being (Chapter Eleven): After you have completed the previous exercise, what have you learned that might help you move forward? Be very honest and precise.

Top Five Characteristics of an Ideal Job or Activity (Chapter Eleven): A chance to be proactive and specific about what you really want to do with your life.

Main Opportunities Your Weaker Characteristics Present You (Chapter Eleven): What you currently consider a weakness or negative characteristic can also be a strength or positive attribute when it is tied to a clear goal. Be careful of this exercise. It means getting rid of your long-time crutches and excuses!

Three Main Occupations/Professional Activities You Would Most Like to Pursue for the Rest of Your Life (Chapter Eleven): Based on some of your previous findings and your defined Ideal Life, write down three substantial activities that will help you realize your dreams. Then write down three reasons why you want to do the first activity on your list. Really narrow it down!

Eleven-Word Epitaph (Chapter Thirteen): Write your own Epitaph as you would like it to appear on your gravestone; the best summary of your life lived. Keep it to eleven words. This requires more thought and precision!

Your Obituary (Chapter Thirteen): Write your own Obituary as you would like it to appear in the local newspaper when the time comes, focusing on any accomplishments, strengths, skills, and qualities that might have added to your life between now and then, along with relationships and what you might be most proud of. Now go out and live it!

Sub-personality Management Techniques

Personal Process Analysis (Chapter Seven): This involves identifying those negative programmes or memes that are heavily ingrained in our unconscious and switching them off or substituting them with new and better ones. By learning to manage our memes, we can regain control of our mental processes and steer them in a way that is beneficial, rather than harmful.

3, 2, 1 Reviewing (Chapter Nine): After a significant event or challenging social encounter (run-in), try to think of three things that went right, that were positive about the situation, and why. Then think of two things that went wrong and why. Finally, find one thing you are determined to change or do differently next time. By learning from experiences in your life, you will ensure more rapid growth in your abilities, competence, and confidence. Try 3, 2, 1 Reviewing at least once a day! With 365 deliberate attempts to get better, you are bound to become a wiser, more skilled human being.

Plan, Act, Review, Improve (PARI) (Chapter Nine): Before an event, such as a get-together with someone who causes a certain amount of emotional or psychological confusion, actively Plan what you hope to get out of the meeting. Armed this way, you should try to Act accordingly. Afterward, you should Review what transpired as carefully as possible and try to come up with possible actions to Improve future encounters.

Internal Travelogue (Chapter Twelve): Going to the different places in our brains to check out our meme flora and fauna. What's dwelling in there? Mind you, it's not always easy to access some of them, they are so deeply buried or ingrained or familiar.

Trial and Success Learning (Chapter Twelve): Some learning, like Personal Process Analysis, is based on identifying what doesn't work, what not to do, or what to avoid in the future, whereas Trial and Success Learning helps us to identify what works and shows us what to do in life. By deliberately and consciously focusing on and pointing out our own and others' successes, strengths, and achievements, we can take advantage of them and learn from them.

Five Skills, Strengths, and Qualities of Others (Epilogue): Before meeting with a "difficult" person, think of Five SSQs he or she might have—positive ones. This will give you a more optimistic outlook. Empower you. We generally aren't taught the techniques to prepare ourselves emotionally and psychologically for most of the challenges thrown our way, but they can be acquired—with effort.

Creative Thinking and Living Techniques

Observation for Awareness (Chapter Twelve): Most of us don't use our senses to their best advantage—or ours. We need to harness all that sensory power to help us go through life more effectively. For example, sight isn't just the physical act of seeing. It is also one route to perception and understanding. Perceiving requires more awareness and consciousness than mere physical seeing.

Real Listening (Chapter Twelve): While most people listen, they are usually just waiting for the other person to stop talking so that they can leap in with their own two cents' worth. The real purpose of conversation should be to form a bridge with another person in order to move the two of you to a new and better place.

First Five Words (Chapter Twelve): The way you go into a conversation is more important than most people realize. Try paying attention to the first five words spoken by you and whomever you are speaking with. They reveal a lot about what will follow and are highly underrated clues in the game of life.

Yes, but . . . Yes, and . . . (Chapter Twelve): We should pay more attention to how sentences are started. The words "Yes, but . . ." indicate a more competitive mind-set, whereas "Yes, and . . ." are more co-operative. Being aware of this provides an easy tool to change one's automatic, negative programming to something more positive. By starting a dialogue with existing points of agreement, you will make it much easier for the other person to handle the points on which you disagree.

Four-Column Chart (Chapter Twelve): One column itemizes your Observations of what has occurred; the next your Interpretations—what caused whatever happened? what was the source or motivation? Then there is the "What Has To Be Done?"

column, listing possible follow-up actions; and finally, "How to Do It," how to carry out whatever has to be done. All this is designed to help people deal with emotional concerns in a more scientific way, not blindly reacting and never solving problems.

Compassing Alternatives (Chapter Twelve): The best alternative is usually in an entirely different direction from what you think it might be. Put your problem down on paper and then look north, south, west, and east for realistic, viable solutions or alternatives. Think creatively, out of the box. If you want to go to Rome, for example, you don't just have to hop on a plane at Heathrow Airport and fly directly to Rome. You could go via Toronto, Tokyo, or even Timbuktu. There are always choices!

APPENDIX B

Characteristics of an Ideal Human Being

Rate Yourself from 1 (Lowest) to 5 (Highest)

Compassionate	Synthesizes Ideas
Loving	Identifies Skills, Strengths, and Qualities
Enthusiastic	Caring
Recognizes Talents	Determined
Trusting	Courageous
Trustworthy	Motivated
Honest	Willing to Learn
Truthful	Considerate
Respectful	Wise
Generous	Resourceful
Listens	Sharing
Purposeful	Learns from Success
Innovative	Positive
Thoughtful	Value-Driven
Creative	Breaks Assumptions
Supportive	Stands Up for Values
Sensitive	Cooperative
Shows Feelings	Has Integrity

Relates to People
Intelligent
Inventive
Decisive
Conceptualizes
Principled
Observant
Note-Taker
Reliable
Giving
Strong
Brave
Kind
Empathetic
Tenacious
Energetic
Confident
Imaginative
Open
Lateral Thinker
Clever
Brilliant
Patient
Has Enthusiasm for Life
Fun
Humorous
Charming
Witty

Modest
Has Positive Self-Worth
Has Belief in Others
Selfless
Joyous
Imparts Hope
Faithful
Loyal
Charitable
Ambitious
Sees Best in Others
Leader
Systematic
Motivational
Dependable
Dedicated
Realistic
Rational
Clear
Challenges
Risk-Taker
Encouraging
Constructive
Helpful
Affirmative
Praises Others
Articulate
Accepting

ACKNOWLEDGEMENTS

I am delighted that my thoughts and efforts have actually resulted in a full-length book. Of course, there were plenty of hurdles along the way for this first-time author—phone messages unanswered, emails ignored, originally signing with the wrong publisher. But there was also a whole lot of support. It's the latter I celebrate here!

First, I want to thank my darling daughter, Wren Montgomery, who has long insisted that her Woo could do so much more; my mother, Ann O'Hara, for listening to the first jet-lag-generated chapters, offering kind suggestions; my lawyer/writer brother Will, who knew what I was going through; my sister Deirdre, who helps me deal with the past; my sister Jill Aslin, who told me my words were therapeutic; and my brother Chris Aslin, who, with his partner Catherine Skene, provided me with an "office" and more.

I owe much to my uncle Brit and aunt Sally for their spirit and support; my nephews and nieces, especially Bronwen and Charlotte O'Hara, for their young wisdom; CJ Stoness for my very positive first review; Allan Mather for his veranda and energy; and Lawrence Martin for *Harperland* and Manhattans. The dedicated Mel Hurtig shared his years' worth of publishing expertise; courageous Paul Hellyer discussed self-publishing over tea and cookies; and Helga Mankovitz has been a generous and understanding fellow prison-farm supporter.

Thanks also to Lori, Jimmy, Mocha, and Chili for being my UK family; Leila Redpath for her poetic way of living; John Browning for inspiring GG's romanticism; Simon Reynier for his gentle kindness; Elizabeth and Jenny Gray for Hampstead; Sinead and Patrick for Spain; Nick Davies, Rick Senley, John Rees, Wendy Kirby, Bruce Kent, Louise Barrington, Jane Crispin, Roy Madron, Ben Perl, Ed Posey, Sulemana Abudulai, Charles Lewis, Janusz Finder, Deb and Harold Frankel, Christopher McTavish, and others for opening up their London;

Hats off to anyone and everyone who simply asked, "How's your book coming along?" or offered to help. If they only knew what that means to a writer! In Kingston, they include: Jamie Sifton, Oscar Malan of Novel Idea, Carolyn Smart, Stuart Ross, Merilyn Simonds, Wayne Grady, Bruce Kauffman, Karilene Montgomery, Susie Bews, Michael Owen-Clark, talented, kind-hearted Louise Stalker and the gang at The Common Market, my aunts Gwen and Cynthia, and dear Ron Turney, who has been there, almost unconditionally, providing me with emotional—and technical—support.

I would like to recognize Victor Navasky and the valiant "crew" of *The Nation* magazine, my Issues Network colleagues, rabble.ca, Charlotte Mundy, Don Allard, Pauline Craydon, Aref Hakki, Elizabeth Gaynes, Ed Finn, Duncan Cameron, John Urquhart, Kingsley and Helen Roby, and host-par-excellence Jim Haynes.

Once I decided to self-publish, former Kingston city counsellor Vicki Schmolka kindly turned her thoughtful legal mind to polishing my words, ideas, and strategies; Anthony Aird offered design suggestions; R. G. Johnston and David More provided details and optimism about going it alone, and the staff at Xlibris were friendly and helpful.

Although she would have preferred me to stick with a Canadian publisher—my preference, too—Anita Purcell of the Canadian Authors Association shared her invaluable insights during lengthy phone conversations, showing me how satisfying, even profound editing can be.

There is one person who truly made *Lost and Found in London* what it is: author/editor Maureen Garvie. She responded to my request for help with such generosity, reshaping my manuscript for the price of a mojito—and basically teaching me how to write a book! Throughout the ups and downs, she kept me going. Thank you isn't enough.

Lastly, there is Chris Coverdale, who took me in, fed me, and informed me. He not only gave me the strength and confidence to write this book and change my life, but also gave me permission to share his ideas and theories with readers. He is out there trying to heal this world; the planet needs many more like him.

ABOUT THE AUTHOR

(Wren Montgomery)

Kathleen O'Hara was the first child of Bill O'Hara, a World War II veteran and Queen's University student, and Ann Smith, football cheerleader and fellow student, in Kingston, Ontario, Canada. After attending elementary and secondary school, as well as university, in her hometown, she moved to and worked in Toronto, Ottawa, Paris, and London with three hot winters in Mexico. She has been employed by government, a political party, non-governmental organizations, and the media. For fifteen years, she has been a columnist with the Issues Network and, more recently, has appeared in *www.rabble.ca*. She has one daughter now working toward her PhD. Kathleen's website address is www.kathleenohara.ca.

CPSIA information can be obtained at www.ICGtesting.com
Printed in the USA
LVOW081330180212

269224LV00001B/31/P

9 781465 338549